Chili Nation

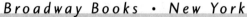
Broadway Books · New York

Chili Nation

The Ultimate

Chili Cookbook

with Recipes from

Every State in

the Nation

Jane & Michael Stern

J

BROADWAY

Broadway Books titles may be purchased for business or promotional use or for special sales. For information, please write to: Special Markets Department, Random House, Inc., 1540 Broadway, New York, NY 10036.

BROADWAY BOOKS and its logo, a letter B bisected on the diagonal, are trademarks of Broadway Books, a division of Random House, Inc.

Library of Congress Cataloging-in-Publication Data
Stern, Jane.
      Chili nation : the ultimate chili cookbook with recipes from
   every state in the nation / Jane and Michael Stern.
          pages   cm.
      Includes index.
      ISBN 0-7679-0263-7 (paper)
      1. Chili con carne.   2. Cookery—United States.
   I. Stern, Michael, 1946–   .   II. Title.
   TX749.S75   1999
   641.8′23—dc21   98-22205
                                                               CIP

FIRST EDITION

Designed by Ralph Fowler

99   00   01   02   10   9   8   7   6   5   4   3

Contents

Acknowledgments   ix

Introduction   1

Fundamental Tips and Tricks   4

Mail-Order Sources   8

Types of Chiles   11

Chili Cook-offs   14

Recipes

ALABAMA
Chili à la Whistle Stop   18

ALASKA
Line Camp Chili and Biscuits   21

ARIZONA
Sonoran Pork, Poblano, and Cream Cheese Chili   24

ARKANSAS
Hot Springs Chili-Tamale Spread   26

CALIFORNIA
Gilroy Super Garlic Chili   30

COLORADO
Venison Chili with Snowcap Beans   33

CONNECTICUT
Herb Garden Springtime Chili   36

DELAWARE
Blue Hen Succotash Chili   38

DISTRICT OF COLUMBIA
Serious Capitol Punishment Chili   40

FLORIDA
Havana Moon Chili   42

GEORGIA
Georgia Pork and Peanut Chili   44

HAWAII
Paniolo Macadamia Nut and Chipotle Chili   46

IDAHO
Chili Coeur d'Alene   48

ILLINOIS
Chicagoland Chili Mac   51

INDIANA
Sunday Supper Chicken Chili   53

IOWA
Tall Corn Pork Chili   56

KANSAS
Porubsky's Grocery Store Chili   58

KENTUCKY
Bluegrass Burgoo Chili   62

LOUISIANA
Mardi Gras Vegetable Chili   65

MAINE
American Chop Suey Chili   68

MARYLAND
Chesapeake Bay Chili   71

MASSACHUSETTS
Rock-Ribbed Bean-and-Beef Chili   73

MICHIGAN
Cornish Miner Chili Pasties   75

MINNESOTA
Café Brenda Black Bean Vegetable Chili   78

MISSISSIPPI
Highway 61 Chili   82

MISSOURI
Mule-Kicking Hot Chili   84

MONTANA
Working Person's Green Chili Bowl   86

NEBRASKA
Church Supper Chili Mac and Cheese   89

NEVADA
Cowboy Poetry Chili   93

NEW HAMPSHIRE
Yankee Bean Pot Chili   95

NEW JERSEY
Chili of the Garden State   98

NEW MEXICO
Mesilla Valley Bowl of Green   100

NEW YORK
Buffalo Beef and Weck Chili   104

NORTH CAROLINA
Pig Chili   106

NORTH DAKOTA
Forty Below Meat Loaf and Mashed Potatoes Chili   108

OHIO
Cincinnati Five-Way Chili   111

OKLAHOMA
16-Times World Champion Sirloin Chili   115

OREGON
Let 'er Buck Red Beer Chili   118

PENNSYLVANIA
Homage to Hershey Chocolate Chili   120

RHODE ISLAND
Chicken Chili and Cornmeal Parsley Dumplings   122

SOUTH CAROLINA
Low-Country Chicken Chili   125

SOUTH DAKOTA
Roughneck Boilermaker Chili   128

TENNESSEE
Memphis Barbecue Shrimp Chili   130

TEXAS
Tigua Indian Definitive Bowl of Red   132

UTAH
Navajo Lamb and Golden Hominy Chili   134

VERMONT
Maple Spiked Chili with Cheddar Stars   136

VIRGINIA
Shenandoah Valley Apple-Nut Chili   139

WASHINGTON
Seattle Coffee Chili   142

WEST VIRGINIA
Fried Bologna Chili   144

WISCONSIN
Green Bay Chili   146

WYOMING
Code 10 Chili   150

Side Dishes

Perfect Simple Guacamole   154
Three-Bean Salad   155
Corn Pudding   156
Jalapeño Corn Bread   157
Coleslaw   158

Index   159

Acknowledgments

Too many cooks may spoil a broth, but chili ain't no wimpy broth. As we wrote this book, eating as well as cooking became an ongoing social event, the more people involved, the merrier. We have had a ball with friends, old and new, as we chopped onions, seeded peppers, stirred pots, and—most important—ate bowl after bowl of chili that needed testing and retesting. For their adventurous palates and willingness to be culinary testers, we thank John Porto, Karen Rue, George Radovan, Jim and Linda Rains, Gael Westphal, Priscilla Lightcap, Aime Stamberg, Eric Nicholson, Victor and Tina Miller, and Rudy and Sally Ruggles.

Thanks also go to the chilihead team at Broadway Books: to editor Harriet Bell and Alexis Levenson and to publisher Bill Shinker; and as always, to our four-alarm agent, Binky Urban.

Jane and Michael Stern

Chili is fun food—easy to make, simple to serve, and a delight to share with friends and family. As American as a cheeseburger, it is appreciated by epicures and chowhounds alike; and perhaps more than any other single dish, its character can vary from rugged to elegant, and its calorie count can go from stout to svelte.

In a quarter century on the road hunting for good things to eat, we have savored gourmet chilies crafted by four-star urban chefs as well as humble ones cooked by night-shift cooks in highway diners. We have spooned up good chili elbow-to-elbow with truck drivers in Tucumcari, New Mexico, and with debutantes in Darien, Connecticut. As home cooks ourselves, we have served chili to friends and neighbors, who range from adventurous omnivores to comfort-food Milquetoasts.

We have come to believe that chili may just be this country's one truly shared national food. Although Tex-Mex in origin, it is a dish now found on every American table, across cultural and ethnic lines.

Its modest beginnings in San Antonio predate the Republic of Texas. Historians speculate that Mexican families living there stewed beef with peppers not only to stretch the quantity but, in the same way other cultures use curry spices, to disguise the taste of less-than-fresh provisions. After the Civil War, chili became identified with the "chili queens" of San Antonio's *mercado,* an anything-goes outdoor bazaar, where Texicans could dine on tamales, enchiladas, and bowls of chili con carne. The queens were colorful women in festively embroidered peasant blouses; and most contemporary accounts make a point of their virtue, despite a reputation for flirting with customers. Still, by the time the chili queens and their wares were banished for health-code reasons in 1943, Texas-style chili had developed an enduring reputation as a red-hot meal at the edge of dining respectability.

Meanwhile, in the Midwest, a whole other school of chili making had been established, mostly by middle European immigrants who added their own panoply of spices to the Texas dish; and in several cities, it was reconfigured entirely to include beans, spaghetti noodles, and oyster crackers (all unheard-of in chili con carne south of the Red River). Typically, midwestern chili was served in open-all-night joints, like the one Edward Hopper depicted in *Night Hawks;* and its image was as food for those of plebeian taste.

Chili's reputation has risen tremendously in recent years. It is no longer looked down on as strictly greasy-spoon fare, a fact that became apparent to us in the early 1990s, when *The New Yorker* assigned us to write a long piece about chili's new respectability, even trendiness. We Americans have become proud of our best blue-collar chow (witness the apotheosis of barbecue and Buffalo chicken wings); and southwestern food in particular has found recognition as a rich culinary heritage.

Newfound respectability does not mean chili has lost its in-your-face personality or its punch. Even when they are not the four-alarm hot variety, most chilies we've encountered in our travels pack a lot of flavor. Indeed, the range of character from coast to coast is tremendous, from the fiery Code 10 Chili we discovered in a small café in Cody, Wyoming, to the honest farm-stand Blue Hen Succotash Chili of Delaware and from the booming Line Camp Chili of Alaska to the health-conscious Black Bean Vegetable Chili of Café Brenda in Minneapolis.

Some kinds of chili have cult followings—in Cincinnati, kaleidoscopic Five-Way Chili is a passion among local connoisseurs, who can tell you which day of the week and what time of day the chili is best at their favorite chili parlor. Some chilies are taken for granted because they are so much a part of culinary custom. In the Mesilla Valley of New Mexico, hardly any meal would be served without a classic bowl of red or bowl of green to accompany whatever else is on the menu. The beauty of these chilies is their absolute simplicity: pureed local peppers, spiced only to accent their flavor, with no meat or starch to dilute the intensity. And there are some chilies that are unknown to the rest of the world but are a true expression of regional gastronomic passion, such as Gilroy Super Garlic Chili from California's farmland, and Cornish Miner Chili Pasties from Michigan's Upper Peninsula.

Many of this book's recipes reflect the specialties of locally cherished chili joints, such as Charlie Porubsky's chili from Porubsky's Grocery of Topeka,

Kansas, and Green Bay Chili from Chili John's of Green Bay, Wisconsin (in business since 1913). Other recipes, while not inspired by a particular restaurant, express the way locals like to eat, incorporating regional produce and flavors, for example, Indiana's Sunday Supper Chicken Chili made with farm-fresh vegetables, Yankee Bean Pot Chili from New Hampshire, and picadillo-like Havana Moon Chili from the Florida Keys.

Chili can be rib sticking or utterly dietetic; it can be made with any or all kinds of meat or no meat at all, with or without beans, fire hot or cream mild. Even the most deluxe recipes are nonintimidating. Creating a breathtaking bowl of red involves little in the way of advanced kitchen skills or exotic ingredients. For spices and chiles that may not be accessible in ordinary markets, we have included a list of mail-order sources (pages 8–10); and we have also included some brief tips for vital chili-specific cooking techniques, such as handling hot peppers and using masa harina to thicken a brew (page 6).

What's especially enjoyable about chili is that every part of this nation has its own way of making it; some versions are so eccentric that people in other regions wouldn't even recognize them. The aim of this book is to take readers and cooks on a coast-to-coast trip to taste the cultural diversity we Americans express in our chili bowls.

Chili is simple to make but awesome to eat. In that sense, it is a dish with the power to make even the most timid cook feel like a master chef. Most of the recipes in this book can be prepared successfully by anyone who can chop an onion and stir a soup. Beyond such basic skills, there are a few additional chili-specific procedures worth knowing. None is difficult, and each is described in some detail when a recipe calls for it; but here they are in longer form, for easy reference.

Rehydrating dried peppers

Dried chiles are an invaluable way to get true chile flavor when you can't get fresh chile peppers. Where we live, in Connecticut, this is true most of the year. So we rely on dried chiles. They are available in well-stocked markets or you can order them by mail (pages 8–10). If you like to cook chili, the ease of collecting a battery of dried anchos, chipotles, and pasillas, all ready to reconstitute, makes life truly delicious. With some dried peppers and a food processor, you are halfway to great chili.

The process is simple. Put as many dried chiles as you need for the recipe in a heatproof bowl. Pour boiling water on top of them. They'll want to float, which is fine, but you can use a heatproof plate or pan lid to keep them underwater. Let them soak about 30 minutes, until they are soft.

Put on a pair of rubber gloves. We like the disposable surgical gloves sold in medical-supply stores or drugstores because they allow you to feel what you are doing, unlike bulky household rubber gloves. Some kind of rubber glove is *absolutely essential* for handling chiles; otherwise, their oils will cling to your fingers for hours, and if you touch your eyes or any other sensitive part of your—or anybody else's—body, the pain can be excruciating. Scrubbing with soap doesn't help much to remove the oil. This warning is particularly important for anyone who wears contact lenses.

Wearing the rubber gloves, pull the stem off each softened pepper and tear the pepper open. Remove all the seeds. The remaining fleshy wall of the pepper pod is then put into a food processor along with some liquid and pureed: essence of chile! Throw the gloves away after use.

NOTE: Pretty though they may be, most chile *ristras* (wreaths or hanging clusters made from dried chiles) are *not* suitable for use in recipes that call for dried chiles. Many are sprayed with shellac to preserve their color or with bug repellent; and those that are not treated often do house insects.

Soaking and cooking dried beans

For chili recipes in which beans are a featured flavor, it's worth the time it takes to soak and cook dried ones.

First, wash them, then let them soak in plenty of cold water, discarding any that float or look moldy. There may also be a stone or two to be discarded. Beans should be soaked 6 to 8 hours or overnight, rinsed, then boiled in fresh water and simmered until tender, generally about 1 hour. When first brought to a simmer, some beans will produce a foam that should be skimmed from the top of the pot. Beans may also be cooked in a pressure cooker. Most beans will be cooked in 10 to 15 minutes.

A quicker way to soak beans—although bean purists say the texture suffers—is to cover dried beans with cold water, bring the water to a boil, and boil 2 minutes. Remove the pot from the heat and let the beans stand in the hot water, covered, for 1 hour. Then cook them at a simmer until tender.

Roasting fresh peppers

Few foods smell as distinctive as roasting chile pepper pods. Earthy and pungent, roasted peppers are, in fact, a favorite roadside snack during chile harvest time in New Mexico: fresh out of the roaster, they are stemmed and seeded on the spot and placed between slabs of rough-grained bread to make a delicious sandwich.

If you have fresh peppers, roasting them can take some effort, but that toasty flavor is a wondrous addition to many chili recipes. The trick is to roast them directly under a hot broiler or over an open flame. (Some tool-happy chefs actually use a blowtorch.) You need to be absolutely vigilant as you do this, for the goal is to blacken the skin but not burn the flesh of the pod. Therefore, the roasting chiles need to be tended constantly and turned as they cook so they are blackened evenly. Once they are blackened, remove them from the flame and wrap each pepper in a damp paper towel. This will quicken their cooling so they can be handled and help you peel off the skin. The skin should come off easily. At this point, once they are peeled, it is best *not* to wash the peppers, as you will wash away some of their flavor. Split them open, remove the stem and seeds, and they are ready to be used in a recipe . . . or to be eaten immediately.

NOTE: As was cautioned in regard to dried chiles, if the peppers you are roasting, peeling, and seeding have any heat whatsoever, *wear rubber gloves when handling them* to avoid getting fiery chile oil on your fingers. Only when handling mild bell peppers can this warning be ignored.

Using masa harina as a thickener

Chili varies in character from stewlike to soupy, but in no case should the liquid be water thin. The classic thickener for chili's broth is 1 or 2 tablespoons of masa harina—corn flour—mixed with a bit of water and added to the pot. Cook and stir the chili a few minutes, and the masa will tighten it, as well as add a pinch of its unique southwestern corn flavor.

Masa harina is found in the flour section of most supermarkets.

What kind of oregano to use

Many recipes in this book specify *Mexican* oregano. The usual oregano on supermarket spice shelves is Italian oregano, which has a slightly different flavor. Mexican oregano has a stronger, more southwestern zest, but if you don't have any (see pages 8–10 for mail-order sources), Italian oregano will work.

Roadhouse Barbecue Sauce

A handful of recipes in this book call for barbecue sauce. Use your favorite, but let us assure you there is none finer than Chicago's Roadhouse brand. If you don't live near a market that sells it, call Mo Hotta-Mo Betta (page 9) or Spices, Etc. (800) 827–6373 and order a few bottles. You may become a convert too.

Scalding fresh tomatoes for easy peeling

When a recipe calls for chopped fresh tomatoes, scald each tomato for 1 minute in boiling water, which makes it easy to pull off its skin before chopping it. Otherwise, pieces of the skin will slip off the diced tomato as the chili cooks and become an annoying texture among the ingredients.

Tomatillos: fresh and canned

For convenience' sake, the recipes in this book that call for tomatillos all specify *canned* tomatillos. If you have fresh ones, they can be substituted by removing the outer paper husk and washing them well before use.

What to cook chili in

Because most chilies in this book are one-dish meals, the recipes here make fairly large quantities (generally enough to feed six people). Therefore, in most cases we suggest cooking the chili in a Dutch oven, which is a capacious cast-iron pan that has a top. Even if using a large skillet, we recommend a heavy one, preferably cast iron, as most chilies require the long, slow simmer that cast iron facilitates.

Coyote Café General Store
132 West Water Street, Santa Fe, NM 87501
(505) 982–2454

A deluxe store attached to chef Mark Miller's high-fashion southwestern restaurant, Coyote Café has a tremendous inventory of chili-related products, including hundreds of hot sauces and colorful posters of chile peppers. Catalog available.

Green Market
Route 4, P.O. Box 870, Quechee, VT 05059
(802) 457–3641

A fun farm stand that is not chile specific, the Green Market is our source for maple pepper, to which we've become mildly addicted for all sorts of things, including the Yankee-theme chili recipe in this book.

Hoppin' John's Book Store
30 Pinckney Street, Charleston, SC 29401
(803) 577–6404

This mecca for all who like to read about cooking and eating also sells a select group of regional food products, including Hoppin' John's grits, ground from whole grain. For the creamy grits recipe on page 126, they're the best you can use. In fact, we've found that many chilies are benefited by the companionship of grits, either freshly made or chilled, cut into squares, and grilled to make crusty corn cakes.

Mo Hotta-Mo Betta

P.O. Box 4136, San Luis Obispo, CA 93403

(800) 462–3220

Spices, chiles, sauces, and salsas from around the world. The catalog, written by serious chiliheads, is loads of fun and as colorful as its name.

Chile Today-Hot Tamale

2-D Great Meadow Lane

E. Hanover, NJ 07936

(800) 468–7377

The best source on earth for all dried chiles as well as chili powders, from mild to super-hot.

Pendery's

304 East Belknap, Fort Worth, TX 76102

(817) 332–3871

Our prime source for dried chiles, chili powders (including hard-to-find green jalapeño powdered chile), masa harina, and rare herbs and spices. They also carry dried vegetables, spiced nuts, and chile-theme novelties galore. Pendery's has a thick catalog inscribed, "Welcome to the World of Chiles and Spices."

Penzeys, Ltd.

P.O. Box 933, Muskego, WI 53150

(414) 679–7207

Penzeys carries exotic spices and herbs from all over the world, including just about anything you'd need for making chili. They have all of the whole dried peppers needed for this book's recipes, as well as powdered peppers and crushed peppers, and a selection of chili powders in varying degrees of hotness. A quarterly catalog is available.

Vermont Country Store

Box 3000, Manchester Center, VT 05255–3000

(802) 362–2400

A fabulous source for all sorts of household arcana, not limited to things culinary. For chili making, the Vermont Country Store has a big inventory of dried beans of every size and color, Vermont Cheddar cheeses for grating on top, and Common Crackers, which are excellent for crumbling into a chili bowl. A catalog is available.

Types of Chiles

From the time Christopher Columbus mistook Hispaniolan *capsicums* for a form of black pepper plant and named them accordingly, chile "peppers" have had an uncertain identity. Even experts aren't clear about what they are: botanists think of the chile as a berry of the nightshade family, like the tomato; agronomists consider it a fruit; New Mexico has declared it an official state vegetable. Spelled at least three different ways (*chili* and *chilli* are alternates), *chile* is the word that refers to the fruit of a plant, whether fresh, dried, crushed, or powdered. *Chili* refers to the dried spice mixture and the one-dish meal.

Chili Nation contains recipes for chili the dish, but each of these recipes contains chili powder and/or chiles, the fruit of *capsicum* plants.

It is crucial to note that *chili powder,* an ingredient in many of these chilies, varies tremendously in flavor as well as heat. We strongly recommend getting a high-quality chili powder from a spice specialist or mail-order source (pages 8–10). If dealing with a company that features chili products, you will find they make several different chili powder blends that vary in heat and flavor. Get some of each, and taste them to see which you like best for various purposes.

Here are thumbnail portraits of the types of chiles used most often in this book. Each is accompanied by its rating in Scoville units (S.U.), which gives a good approximation of its hotness. (Chiles vary considerably in this respect from crop to crop.) A rating of 0 is totally not hot: green bell pepper, for instance. The scale goes to 300,000 units for habanero peppers, as hot as it gets.

Anaheim
(1,000 S.U. = mild)

Generally quite mild, the Anaheim is a large, thick-fleshed pepper with a sunny vegetable flavor. It is available both green and red (ripened). The ripened Anaheim is quite sweet, like a bell pepper with a more assertive personality.

Ancho
(3,000 S.U. = fairly hot)

The ancho is a dried poblano chile with a deep, leathery flavor and moderate heat. There is a certain fruity zest to the ancho that makes it essential in Mexican *mole* and gives many chili dishes their buoyant charm.

Chipotle
(15,000 S.U. = quite hot)

A dried, smoked jalapeño, the chipotle has an earthy aroma that is a siren song to serious chiliheads. Usually fairly hot, it is a fundamental element of many fiery southwestern bowls of red; and its distinctive smoky-sweet flavor becomes a dominant note in almost any dish in which it's used.

Habanero
(300,000 S.U. = painfully hot)

About as hot as chiles get, the habanero is strictly for chile maniacs, and then only in itty-bitty pieces as a condiment. Unless you really like four-alarm food, avoid it. But if you do like your chili hot, a little bit of finely minced habanero pepper—or a dash of salsa or hot sauce made from habaneros—will provide not only heat but also the unusual tropical zest that no other pepper provides.

Jalapeño
(10,000 S.U. = pretty damn hot)

The jalapeño is genuine hot stuff, but not unbearable to most tongues. In the raw, it is a favorite munching garnish to accompany Texas bowls of red or plates of barbecue. It is also served pickled and sliced, and generally used as a garnish for plates of super-nachos or green-chile cheeseburgers. The jalapeño has a powerful garden flavor as well as heat.

New Mexico
(1,000 S.U. = mild)

Also known as the long green, the New Mexico chile varies in heat level from mild to medium-hot. It is large and thick fleshed and has a summer-sun flavor that makes connoisseurs of New Mexican food declare it the most delicious pepper of all. Simply roasted and peeled, it is a snack-food staple from the Mesilla Valley in the south to the foothills of the Sangre de Cristos. Pureed long greens—or their ripened red incarnation—are frequently served in bowls alongside other meals as a dip for warm flour tortillas.

Pasilla
(5,000 S.U. = good and hot)

A dark, dried pepper also known as *chile negro*. Medium hot, it has a beguiling fruity taste that makes it a favorite to puree as the basis of more complicated chili recipes.

Poblano
(±3,000 S.U. = hot)

So dark green it may appear black, the poblano chile ranges from just moderately hot to three alarm. It has thick-fleshed walls, making it wonderful for roasting, which brings out its profound, verdant flavor.

Chili Cook-offs

C hili cook-offs take place throughout the year and all over the country (as well as the world) and provide an opportunity for connoisseurs not only to compete, compare, and contrast but also to have a chili-themed party. If these cook-offs are any indication, chiliheads are boisterous sorts of people; and it has been traditional since the modern cook-off era began in Terlingua, Texas, in 1967, for contestants to include massive amounts of swagger and braggadocio along with their recipes. To put it kindly, a chili cook-off tends not to be a contemplative culinary event.

The big organization that sponsors the cook-offs is the International Chili Society (ICS), which—in typically grandiose chilihead fashion—bills itself as "the largest food contest festival organization in the world." The ICS puts its imprimatur on some three hundred local, regional, and international cook-offs each year and on the World's Championship Chili Cook-off the first week of October. Their "sole purpose is to promote, develop, and improve the preparation and appreciation of true chili and to determine each year the World's Champion Chili through officially sanctioned and regulated competitive cook-offs. This association shall further the camaraderie of chiliheads on behalf of charitable and non-profit organizations in the world."

The ICS grew out of the Chili Appreciation Society International, a gang of hell-bent-for-leather gents who first got organized in a somewhat quiet fashion in the early 1950s but then started making serious noise in 1967. That year, they came together in south Texas, partly to see who made the best chili, partly to have a big party, and partly to promote the just-published book *A Bowl of Red*, by *Dallas News* columnist Frank X. Tolbert. Tolbert's book, which has since become the bible for chili connoisseurs and an indispensable account of southwestern food lore, is still in print and now contains a full account of the origins of what has become a national culinary sport.

Membership in the ICS costs $30 per year. Members receive a quarterly newspaper that includes sixty pages of chili-related news, photos, and recipes.

For detailed information about upcoming events, how to stage your own officially sanctioned chili cook-off, and how to join, contact

International Chili Society
P.O. Box 2966
Newport Beach, CA 92663
phone: (714) 631–1780
fax: (714) 631–1786

Or check out their Web site at www.chilicookoff.com. There you'll find a history
of the ICS along with prize-winning recipes from the last three decades.

Recipes

Recipes are arranged alphabetically by state.

Note on quantity: Unless otherwise noted, each recipe makes chili for 6 servings.

Note on heat level: The heat of any particular type of chile pepper can vary tremendously from crop to crop. (See pages 11–13 for specific heat ranges.) Rather than rate each recipe on an arbitrary scale of hotness, we have tried to indicate in the headnote the approximate heat range of the recipe; and when appropriate, we have given alternative ingredients for those who like their chili extremely hot or very mild.

Chili à la Whistle Stop

THE IRONDALE CAFÉ WAS ORIGINALLY opened by author Fannie Flagg's great aunt Bess at the train station in the small town of Irondale, just east of Birmingham, Alabama. Ms. Flagg's novel about growing up in and around the café, *Fried Green Tomatoes at the Whistle Stop Café*, became a bestseller and a popular movie; and the café, now owned by the McMichaels family, who bought it from Aunt Bess, is still a great source of honest country cooking at low prices.

Service is cafeteria style, with a different menu each day of the week. There are always several lusciously cooked southern-style vegetables (including fried green tomatoes, of course) to accompany such hearty entrées as meat loaf, fried chicken, country-fried steak, and smothered pork chops.

Whistle Stop chili is a stalwart, gently spiced bowl of food, recommended by Ms. Flagg in her *Whistle Stop Café Cookbook* "if you are sick or it is cold outside." As we've cooked it over the years, we have altered the recipe somewhat but always have kept the one ingredient that makes Whistle Stop chili unique, the unusual inclusion of oatmeal. There isn't enough to seriously thicken the chili, but it does generate a certain velvet texture that soothes the tongue. This is a simple, old-fashioned meal, especially satisfying when served on a bed of broken crackers and eaten with a big spoon. Its heat level is close to zero.

1 cup chopped onions

3 garlic cloves, minced

2 tablespoons vegetable oil

1¼ pounds lean ground chuck

One 14½-ounce can beef broth

One 15-ounce can tomato sauce

One 10-ounce can Ro-tel tomatoes and green chiles, drained

¼ cup uncooked old-fashioned rolled oats

1 teaspoon salt

1 tablespoon sugar

¼ cup chili powder

1 teaspoon red pepper flakes

1 teaspoon ground cumin

Two 15-ounce cans pinto beans, drained

Saltine crackers

Grated cheese

1) In a Dutch oven over medium heat, sauté the onions and garlic in the oil. Add the beef and cook until well browned, stirring to break up the meat. Drain the excess oil.

2) Add the remaining ingredients, except the beans, crackers, and cheese. Bring to a boil; lower the heat, cover, and simmer 40 minutes, stirring occasionally. Add the beans. Simmer, partially covered, 15 minutes more.

3) Serve in a bowl on a bed of crumbled saltine crackers and garnish with the grated cheese.

Line Camp
Chili and Biscuits

CHILI IS ESPECIALLY RIGHT AS A WIN-
ter meal in the wilderness. Simple to make and
serve, as satisfying as a good stew but more excitingly spiced, it has
long been a staple of chuck wagon cooks and adventurers at the edge of
the American frontier. Alaska, which likes to think of itself as the Last
Frontier, is the adopted home of many Texans who headed up to the
North Slope oil country, so it is no surprise that it is a major chili-eating
state with a distinct southwestern accent.

This Alaskan chili is a hearty bowl of red with winter vegetables in
which the chipotle chiles' smart kick is nicely complemented by a
creamy crust of biscuits. No beans are allowed, of course. But if you are
feeling lazy, premade biscuits, found in the refrigerator case of the supermarket, may be substituted for the from-scratch ones suggested here.

This chili is eye-opening hot, but not ferocious.

FOR THE CHILI

4 dried chipotle chiles

4 dried ancho chiles

1 to 1 1/2 cups tomato sauce

1 cup flat beer

1 cup chopped onions

2 garlic cloves, minced

1/4 cup vegetable oil

1 cup sliced carrots, cut into 1/4-inch slices

1 cup sliced parsnips, cut into 1/4-inch slices

1 1/2 pounds sirloin steak, trimmed of fat and cut into 1/2-inch cubes

1 1/2 teaspoons salt

1/2 teaspoon freshly ground black pepper

1 teaspoon ground cumin

1 tablespoon Worcestershire sauce

FOR THE BISCUITS

2 cups all-purpose flour

1 tablespoon baking powder

1/2 teaspoon salt

1/2 teaspoon cream of tartar

2 tablespoons sugar

1/2 cup solid vegetable shortening

2/3 to 3/4 cup milk

Make the chili

1) Place the dried chiles in a large heatproof bowl and cover with boiling water. Let stand 30 minutes, until soft; then seed and stem them. In a food processor, puree the chiles with 1 cup of the tomato sauce and the beer. Set aside.

2) In a deep, heavy skillet or Dutch oven, sauté the onions and garlic in the vegetable oil until the onions begin to soften. Add the carrots and parsnips and sauté until soft, 7 to 10 minutes. Add the beef and stir to brown it.

3) Add the pureed chile mixture to the skillet along with the salt, pepper, cumin, and Worcestershire. Simmer, uncovered, 10 minutes, stirring often, adding only enough of the remaining tomato sauce to keep the chili from sticking. You don't want this chili soupy. Keep it warm while you prepare the biscuits.

Make the biscuits

1) Preheat the oven to 425°F. Mix the flour, baking powder, salt, cream of tartar, and sugar in a large bowl. Cut in the shortening until the mixture is crumbly. Pour in the milk and stir just long enough to make a dough that holds together. On a lightly floured board, knead the dough a dozen times, and no more. Pat the dough out about ³/₄ inch thick. Using a floured drinking glass or a cookie cutter, about 2 inches in diameter, cut the dough into rounds. Reroll the scraps to cut more biscuits. There should be a total of 5 or 6 biscuits.

2) Put the chili into a 2- to 2¹/₂-quart casserole. Top with the biscuits, which will have to be squeezed together to fit in a single layer. Bake about 20 minutes, until the biscuits are light brown. Serve immediately.

Sonoran Pork, Poblano, and Cream Cheese Chili

SOUTHERN ARIZONA'S MEXICAN FOOD is a world apart from Tex-Mex: milder and wheatier, with a color palate that leans less toward the fire reds and spectral oranges of the Rio Grande and more toward mellow green and yellow shades of pale like night flowers in the desert. Although chile peppers are popular on local tables—stuffed as *chiles rellenos* and strewn over quesadillas and chimichangas—a simple bowl of chili, served as a meal, is a rarity.

Inspired by the many beautiful meals we have eaten at the tables of chef Suzanna Davilla at our favorite Arizona restaurant, Café Poca Cosa of Tucson, this pork and poblano chili is lovely to behold: pastel hued and silky, with a gentle toasty flavor and the fine-textured elegance of pork.

5 fresh poblano chilies, roasted, skinned, and seeded (p. 5)

1 cup chicken broth

4 ounces cream cheese (do not use low-fat or whipped cream cheese)

2 garlic cloves, minced

2 tablespoons vegetable oil

2 pounds pork loin, trimmed of fat and cut into $1/2$-inch pieces

1 teaspoon salt

$1/2$ teaspoon green jalapeño powder

Chopped cilantro

Cooked rice

1) Place the roasted peppers, chicken broth, and cream cheese in a food processor or blender. Puree until smooth. Set aside.

2) In a large cast-iron skillet, sauté the garlic in the oil over medium heat until soft. Add the pork and sauté until it is cooked through well browned all over. Add the salt and jalapeño powder along with the chile puree and cook over low heat until just warm. *Do not boil.*

3) Serve, sprinkled with cilantro, over rice.

Hot Springs Chili-Tamale Spread

ARKANSAS COOKS HAVE A WAY WITH food that is such an ingrained part of the culinary culture that few locals, and even fewer outsiders, are aware of how peculiarly Arkansan it is: layering. For reasons we've never fathomed, Razorback food is frequently presented in a pile, one thing atop another. Barbecue salad, for example, is a popular item in which a full-house garden salad serves merely as the base of a heap of warm barbecued meat and sauce and/or salad dressing. The rib and fry plate at McClard's, the state's premier barbecue in Hot Springs, is a massive oval dish on which a full slab of ribs is totally eclipsed by a heap of delicious french fries. McClard's is also known for a unique dish called a spread: a plate of tamales topped with chopped smoked barbecue meat, beans, crisp corn chips, chopped raw onions, and shredded cheese. McClard's spread inspired this similarly layered chili.

If you're lucky enough to have access to good ready-to-go tamales, this Hot Springs Chili-Tamale Spread is the easiest dish in the world to make, demanding only a simple meat-and-bean concoction to top the tamales. Otherwise, you'll have to make your own tamales, as follows. The chili itself will be as zesty as the barbecue sauce you use.

FOR THE TAMALES

3 dozen corn husks (or parchment paper cut into 8 × 5-inch rectangles)

³/₄ pound finely ground beef

1 garlic clove, minced

1 tablespoon bacon fat

¹/₂ cup beef broth

¹/₄ cup chili powder

1 teaspoon ground cumin

2 teaspoons salt

1 cup warm water

3 cups finely ground yellow cornmeal

1 cup lard

Make the tamales

1) Soak the corn husks in hot water until pliable, about 1 hour. (Do not soak the parchment paper.)

2) In a heavy skillet, brown the beef and garlic in the bacon fat. Add the broth, chili powder, cumin, and 1 teaspoon of the salt. Simmer uncovered about 30 minutes, adding more broth, if necessary, to make a thick, moist mixture (a little over 1 cup).

3) Combine the warm water with the cornmeal; let stand until the water is absorbed. Cream the lard with the remaining 1 teaspoon salt until fluffy. Add the cornmeal mixture and beat well. Combine the cornmeal and meat mixtures. Spread 2 tablespoons of the mixture in each husk, leaving a 1-inch margin untouched by filling. Roll up the husks, forming tight wrappers around the filling, and tie each end with twine, an extra husk cut into long strips, or a twist tie.

FOR THE CHILI

1 cup chopped onions

2 garlic cloves, minced

2 tablespoons vegetable or corn oil

1 pound lean ground chuck

2 cups barbecue sauce

1 teaspoon salt

1/4 cup chili powder

1 teaspoon hot red pepper flakes

1 teaspoon ground cumin

Two 15-ounce cans pinto beans, drained

FOR THE SPREAD

1 1/2 cups chopped scallions (white and green parts)

1 1/2 cups (12 ounces) grated American or mild Cheddar cheese

Fritos corn chips, for garnish

4) Pour about 1 inch of water in a pot that is tall and narrow enough to keep the tamales from tipping over. Stand the tamales upright on a rack that holds them above the water. Cover loosely and steam 45 minutes.

Make the chili

1) Sauté the onions and garlic in the oil in a Dutch oven. Add the ground chuck and cook until well browned, stirring to break up the meat. Drain the excess fat.

2) Add the remaining ingredients, except the beans; bring to a boil. Lower the heat, cover, and simmer 40 minutes, stirring occasionally. Add the beans. Simmer, partially covered, 15 minutes more.

Construct the spread

Preheat the oven to 350°F. Butter a broad shallow casserole or two smaller ones (so you have enough space to spread out the tamales in a single layer). Remove the tamales from their husks and layer them on the bottom of the casserole. Top with the chili, a sprinkle of scallions, and a layer of cheese. Bake 20 to 25 minutes, until the cheese begins to brown. Garnish with the corn chips.

Gilroy Super Garlic Chili

THE SMALL TOWN OF GILROY, CALIFOR-
nia, is the Garlic Growing Capital of the World, pro-
ducing hundreds of thousands of tons of aromatic bulbs every year.
The fertile farmland east of Monterey Bay also yields bountiful crops
of tomatoes, onions, and peppers; so when local produce is harvested
and processed, the air smells like an Italian food festival. Humorist Will
Rogers once declared Gilroy "the only town in America where you can
marinate a steak just by hanging it out on the clothesline."

To celebrate its status as Garlic Central, Gilroy initiated an outra-
geous food festival in August 1979 devoted to eating, cooking, and otherwise admiring the world's best-known vampire repellent. Among the
recipes entered in the 1980 cooking contest was an intriguing one from
Wesley L. Minor of Seal Beach, California, for Green Garlic Chili. We
came across it in the locally published *Garlic Lovers' Cookbook*, an entire

volume devoted to things you can make using the stinking rose: from garlic soup to garlic pudding for dessert.

What we like about Mr. Minor's chili is its use of whole garlic cloves, a technique reminiscent of James Beard's famous recipe for Chicken with 40 Cloves of Garlic. Cooked long and slow in olive oil, the garlic cloves lose their bite, soften, and become the chile peppers' amiable companions. The original recipe calls for fresh green chiles as well as green tomatoes. Over the years, we've modified the formula quite a bit. Because we can't always get fresh chiles, we use dried ones—fairly mild California chiles work best in this recipe—and we started using canned tomatillos when we couldn't find green tomatoes.

This chili has enough of a punch that you don't want to serve anything elaborate on the side. We like it best in a bowl with a few boiled potatoes or white rice, or with lengths of sturdy French bread for mopping sauce and using as a bed for the whole cloves of garlic retrieved from the bowl.

6 dried California chiles

One 28-ounce can tomatillos, drained

$^1/_2$ cup olive oil

3 large garlic bulbs, separated into cloves (40 to 50 cloves)

$^1/_2$ cup chopped onions

2 pounds chuck roast, cut into $^1/_2$-inch cubes

$^1/_2$ teaspoon salt

$^1/_4$ teaspoon freshly ground black pepper

1 large tomato, skinned and diced

1 cup chopped fresh basil

1) Place the chiles in a large heatproof bowl and cover with boiling water. Let stand 30 minutes, until soft; then seed and stem them. In a food processor or blender, process or puree the chiles and tomatillos. Set aside.

2) Heat the oil in a heavy skillet. Peel the garlic cloves and sauté them until they are soft and just barely begin to brown. Add the onions and cook until soft. Add the beef, salt, and pepper, stirring to brown the beef on all sides. Pour off the excess fat. Add the chile puree and the tomato. Stir in the basil and simmer uncovered 30 minutes, stirring often.

Venison Chili
with Snowcap Beans

A WHILE BACK, *GOURMET* MAGAZINE asked us to select some of our favorite self-published community cookbooks to share with their readers. This was a real pleasure, because when we travel around the country, we hardly ever leave a place without a trunk full of regional recipes put together by the Junior League, the Elks Club, the Pork Producers, the Cow Belles (wives of cattlemen), the PTA, or the lady who runs the local café who wants to share her culinary discoveries with the world.

One of the best of these cookbooks is called *Colorado Cache*, in which we found an intriguing recipe called Daddy's Venison Chili. We toyed with what Daddy had to offer and came up with a tasty version that expresses the indigenous chili flavors of the Rocky Mountain state. For those without venison or who are averse to game meat, cubes of beef can be used and the chili will still taste fine—hearty and satisfying, but not fire hot.

Note that preparation of the beans should begin the day before making the chili, unless the quick-soak method is used (see page 5).

FOR THE BEANS

16 ounces dried snowcap beans (found in gourmet or health food stores.)

5 garlic cloves

1 tablespoon whole coriander seeds

1 bay leaf

1 tablespoon salt

FOR THE CHILI

8 dried ancho chiles

1 large green bell pepper, seeded and chopped

1 cup chopped onions

3 garlic cloves, minced

4 tablespoons vegetable oil

3 1/2 pounds lean venison (or beef), cut into 1/2-inch cubes

1 1/2 pounds sweet pork sausage, cut into 1-inch cubes

1 tablespoon salt

1 1/2 teaspoons freshly ground black pepper

1 1/2 teaspoons dried Mexican oregano

2 teaspoons ground cumin

2 tablespoons sugar

Two 14 1/2-ounce cans whole tomatoes

2 tablespoons masa harina dissolved in 1/2 cup water

Make the beans

Soak the beans overnight. In the morning, pick out any bad ones and any stones. Wash the beans and place them in a large pot filled with water. Place the garlic, coriander seeds, and bay leaf in a cheesecloth bag or tea ball and add to the beans in the water. Bring the water to a boil, reduce the heat to a simmer, and cook the beans 1 hour, until tender. Discard the spices. Drain the beans well and set aside while you make the chili. Add the salt.

Make the chili

1) Place the chiles in a large heatproof bowl and cover with boiling water. Let stand 30 minutes, until soft; then seed and stem them. In a food processor or blender, puree the chiles with 1 cup water until smooth. Set aside.

2) In a large skillet, brown the bell pepper, onions, and garlic in 2 tablespoons of the oil until they are soft. Set aside.

3) In a large Dutch oven, brown the venison and sausage in the remaining 2 tablespoons of oil. Drain the excess fat. Add the bell pepper mixture along with the salt, pepper, oregano, cumin, sugar, and 3 cups water. Add the tomatoes, smashing each in the palm of your hand before adding it to the pot. Add the chile puree, stir, and bring to a boil. Reduce the heat and cook, partially covered, at a low boil for 1½ hours. Remove from the heat. Add the masa harina mixture, stirring to thicken the chili. Return the chili to the heat and cook 7 more minutes.

4) Serve in deep bowls atop a bed of the snowcap beans.

Herb Garden
Springtime Chili

AMONG CONNECTICUT'S LESSER-KNOWN culinary attractions are all the herbs grown in garden centers around the state. Caprilands Herb Farm of Coventry is an eighteenth-century farmhouse surrounded by more than 50 acres of 30 different gardens, some dizzyingly fragrant and others more beautiful than a field full of butterflies. Catnip Acres Herb Nursery in Oxford grows more than 400 varieties of herbs in their gardens and greenhouses. In Westport, the venerable Gilbertie's Herb Farm is the place to which homemaker supreme Martha Stewart went to learn all she needed to know about growing and using fresh herbs . . . including the fact that the letter *H* is *not* dropped when you say the word *herb*.

If you cannot get fresh herbs, don't even bother with this recipe for herbaceous chili; but if you do have a summer garden or a greenhouse source, it can be a verdant bowl of green that is a rhapsody of nature's flavors. The heat level is low; and as a bonus, it is virtually fat free.

2 tablespoons chopped
fresh marjoram

$^1/_4$ cup snipped fresh
chives

$^1/_2$ cup chopped fresh
flat-leaf Italian parsley

2 tablespoons chopped
fresh oregano

$^1/_2$ cup chopped fresh
basil

1 cup canned tomatillos

One 4$^1/_2$-ounce can mild
green chiles

$^3/_4$ cup chicken broth

3 garlic cloves, minced

$^1/_3$ cup chopped
scallions

2 tablespoons vegetable
oil

2 pounds skinless,
boneless chicken breasts,
cut into $^1/_2$-inch cubes

$^1/_2$ tablespoon sugar

$^1/_4$ teaspoon green
jalapeño powder

Salt to taste

1 tablespoon masa
harina dissolved in
$^1/_4$ cup water

Boiled small spring
potatoes

1) In a food processor or blender, combine the marjoram, chives, parsley, oregano, basil, tomatillos, green chiles, and chicken broth. Pulse until the mixture is a very coarse puree, not smooth. Set aside.

2) In a heavy skillet, sauté the garlic and scallions in the vegetable oil until soft. Add the chicken; sprinkle in the sugar and brown the chicken well. Add the herb puree and jalapeño powder. Cook over low heat for 7 minutes. Taste and add salt as needed. Stir in the masa harina mixture and cook for 4 minutes more, until thickened.

3) Serve with boiled small spring potatoes.

Blue Hen Succotash Chili

BOYHOOD HOME OF FRANK PURDUE, Delaware boasts the chicken as its state bird. In addition to its poultry fame, it is also a big vegetable state and the nation's leading producer of canned lima beans.

In the Blue Hen State, which is Delaware's nickname, we like to poke around the farm stands around New Castle. It is there, in the spring and summer months, that one can find all the fresh produce needed for this mild chicken chili, which is a vegetable lover's delight. (If it's winter, frozen vegetables stand in well.)

²/₃ cup chopped onions

2 garlic cloves, minced

1 cup finely chopped carrots

4 tablespoons olive oil

1 ¹/₂ pounds ground chicken breast

2 cups cooked fresh lima beans, or one 10-ounce package frozen

2 cups corn kernels fresh off the cob, or one 10-ounce package frozen

One 14-ounce can chicken broth

1 teaspoon ground cumin

1 tablespoon chili powder

¹/₂ cup sweet red chile flakes (available from Pendery's)

2 teaspoons salt

1 teaspoon freshly ground black pepper

1 tablespoon sugar

2 cups fresh tomatoes, skinned and diced

2 tablespoons masa harina dissolved in ¹/₄ cup water

1) In a Dutch oven, sauté the onions, garlic, and carrots in 2 tablespoons of the oil until the carrots start to soften. Add the remaining 2 tablespoons of oil and the chicken. Cook, stirring and scraping the pan constantly to keep the chicken broken up, until the chicken is cooked through.

2) Add the beans, corn, broth, cumin, chili powder, chile flakes, salt, pepper, and sugar. Bring to a low simmer and cook, stirring, 7 minutes. Add the tomatoes and cook 3 minutes more. Add the masa harina mixture and cook 5 minutes more.

Serious Capitol Punishment Chili

I N 1980 THE INTERNATIONAL CHILI SOCIETY awarded top prize at its annual cook-off to Bill Pfeiffer of Washington, D.C., for a recipe he called Capitol Punishment.

This recipe was inspired by Mr. Pfeiffer's original. We have upgraded the brand of beer he used, substituted bitter chocolate for the teaspoon of mole (a blend of spices and chocolate) he suggested, and made a few other minor alterations.

What we have not messed with is Mr. Pfeiffer's interesting idea of using both ground and cubed meat together to create an unusual and appealing texture. We were also intrigued by the way this chili is constructed by making a smudge pot of all the spices first and then adding the meat. Although it is vigorously spiced, we believe D.C. chili to be eminently more digestible than anything else inside-the-Beltway folks have asked us to swallow in years.

1 tablespoon dried Mexican oregano

1 tablespoon paprika

4 tablespoons chili powder

$^1/_2$ tablespoon ground cumin

2 tablespoons (2 cubes) beef bouillon

1 tablespoon sugar

1 teaspoon hot sauce

1 tablespoon unsweetened cocoa powder

$^1/_2$ tablespoon hot red pepper flakes

One 12-ounce bottle pale lager ale

1 tablespoon ground coriander

One 14$^1/_2$-ounce can Hunt's diced tomatoes with roasted garlic

1 cup chopped onions

5 garlic cloves, minced

2 tablespoons vegetable oil

1 pound lean beef round, cut into $^1/_4$-inch cubes

$^1/_2$ pound lean ground chuck

$^1/_2$ pound ground pork

2 tablespoons masa harina dissolved in $^1/_2$ cup warm water

1) In a large Dutch oven, combine the oregano, paprika, chili powder, cumin, beef bouillon, sugar, hot sauce, cocoa, pepper flakes, ale, coriander, tomatoes, and 1 cup water. Bring to a boil and remove from the heat.

2) In a large skillet, fry the onions and garlic in the vegetable oil. Add the beef cubes, ground beef, and ground pork; brown and remove from the heat. Drain the excess fat. Add the meat to the "seasoning soup." Stir well and cook, partially covered, 1 hour 15 minutes at a low boil. Remove from the heat, add the masa harina mixture, and cook 2 minutes more over low heat.

Havana Moon Chili

T'S A LONG TRIP FROM ANYWHERE IN the ordinary U.S.A. to the southernmost tip of Florida: Key West. Here in the Conch Republic, you are closer to Havana than to Miami, and the taste of life has a spice all its own.

One of the most alluring things that keeps our car heading south by southwest toward Margaritaville is the promise of the great Cuban-accented food to be savored in Miami and along the overseas highway that threads the Keys. Let others visit Florida to spend time with Mickey Mouse; we'll go for the fried plantains, the guanabana milk shakes, the black beans and rice, and coffee strong enough to make the rooster crow. We also go for the picadillo at El Siboney, our favorite Cuban-style restaurant in Key West.

Picadillo is served all over south Florida. It is a humble ground meat dish that sparkles with the tang of green olives, vinegar, and capers. Our Havana Moon recipe marries the basic elements of picadillo to the spirit and spices of chili making. The result is an easy-to make one-dish meal with chili's satisfaction and a high-spirited Cuban twist.

2 tablespoons vegetable oil

¹/₂ cup chopped onion

3 garlic cloves, minced

1 pound ground pork

1 pound ground chuck

One 14¹/₂-ounce can beef broth

One 28-ounce can whole peeled tomatoes, drained

2 tablespoons balsamic vinegar

¹/₃ cup raisins

2 tablespoons chili powder

1 teaspoon ground cinnamon

1 teaspoon ground cumin

¹/₂ teaspoon ground allspice

¹/₄ teaspoon ground cloves

¹/₂ tablespoon salt

¹/₄ cup pimiento-stuffed green olives, halved

¹/₄ cup slivered blanched almonds

2 cups cooked black beans

2 cups cooked white rice

1) Heat the vegetable oil in a Dutch oven. Stir in the onion and garlic and cook until soft. Add the pork and beef, and cook until browned. Drain off the excess fat.

2) Add the beef broth and tomatoes, squashing each tomato by hand before adding it. Stir in the vinegar, raisins, spices, and salt. Bring to a boil; reduce the heat and cook 30 minutes, partially covered. Uncover and cook for 30 minutes more. Add the olives and almonds and cook an additional 5 minutes.

3) To serve, place a mound of beans and a mound of rice in each bowl. Ladle the chili on top.

Georgia Pork and Peanut Chili

EVER SINCE WE TUCKED INTO PRESI-
dential Pudding at Mary Mac's Tea Room in Atlanta
during Jimmy Carter's term in the White House, we have always asso-
ciated Georgia with good things peanutty. (The dish was named to
honor the Georgian's former vocation as a peanut farmer.) The pudding, aka Carter Custard, is a balmy confection served in a graham
cracker crust and sprinkled with roasted peanuts.

In 1984, the Georgia Peanut Commission published *Peanuts: A
Southern Tradition*, filled with recipes of great things to cook with the
legume, which in fact is not a nut at all, but a member of the bean family. Among the recipes is a tasty dish called Mexican Pork with Peanut
Sauce, which we've adapted to make this chili, which is a marvelous
harmony of peanut's richness and chili's zest. The goobers give the
sauce a grainy texture that makes such a nice envelope for tender pork,
here cut into slices to which the sauce clings so well.

One 2-pound pork
tenderloin roast

8 dried ancho chiles

1 1/3 cups unsalted
shelled peanuts

One 14 1/2-ounce can
diced tomatoes with juice

2 cups tomato sauce

1/2 cup chopped onion

2 garlic cloves, minced

2 tablespoons vegetable
oil

1 teaspoon ground
coriander

1 teaspoon ground
cumin

1 teaspoon salt

1 tablespoon sugar

1 cup chicken broth

Cooked rice

1) Preheat the oven to 350°F. Place the pork in an uncovered roasting pan and roast for about 1 hour, until cooked through. Set aside. When cool enough to handle, slice the pork into 1/4-inch-thick pieces.

2) Place the chiles in a large heatproof bowl and cover with boiling water. Let stand for 30 minutes, until soft; then seed and stem them. Place the chiles, peanuts, tomatoes and their juice, and 1 cup of the tomato sauce in a food processor. Puree thoroughly.

3) In a large heavy skillet or Dutch oven, sauté the onion and garlic in the vegetable oil. Add the chile puree, coriander, cumin, salt, sugar, and pork to the skillet. Stir to mix, adding the remaining 1 cup of tomato sauce and the chicken broth. Cook over low heat, 10 to 15 minutes.

4) Serve with rice.

Paniolo Macadamia Nut and Chipotle Chili

I N HAWAII COWBOYS ARE CALLED PANIO-
los. It wasn't until we met Gene Stowell, a Hawaiian
cowboy, at the Elko, Nevada, Cowboy Poetry Gathering, that we
learned how popular rodeo is in America's westernmost state, where
cattle-country culture is alive and well. Gene is a calf roper, a rodeo an-
nouncer, and a songwriter; and his tales of ranch life in Polynesia inspired this cross-cultural chili recipe.

Macadamia nuts and pork are used often in Hawaiian cooking;
and it is just wonderful how well they marry with the smoky essence of
pureed chipotle chile peppers. This is a quite-hot brew, but its curious
savor is elegant enough for a sophisticated dinner party. The array of
brightly colored Terra vegetable chips on which it is served is as colorful as a floral lei.

4 large dried ancho chiles

4 dried chipotle chiles

1 1/2 cups chicken broth

1/2 cup whole macadamia nuts

2 garlic cloves, minced

1/4 cup chopped onion

2 tablespoons vegetable oil

2 pounds boneless pork, cubed

1 tablespoon salt

1 tablespoon chili powder

2 teaspoons ground coriander

One 6-ounce bag of Terra vegetable chips (These delicate fried chips are made from taro, yuca, sweet potato, ruby taro, batata, and parsnips. They are available at most health food stores and deluxe supermarkets.)

1 cup chopped fresh parsley

1) Place all the chiles in a large heatproof bowl and cover with boiling water. Let stand 30 minutes; then seed and stem them. In a food processor or blender, puree the chiles with 1/2 cup of the chicken broth and the macadamia nuts. Set aside.

2) In a Dutch oven, sauté the garlic and onion in the oil until soft. Add the pork and cook until browned. Drain off any excess fat. Add the chile puree, salt, chili powder, coriander, and the remaining 1 cup of chicken broth. Bring the mixture to a boil; reduce the heat to a slow simmer and cook, uncovered, stirring regularly, for 30 minutes.

3) To serve, place a handful of vegetable chips in the bowl, ladle on the chili, and sprinkle it with the parsley.

Chili Coeur d'Alene

COEUR D'ALENE IS THE HUB OF IDAHO'S panhandle, a vast paradise for outdoor types who like to fish, hunt, camp, and get far away from civilization's constraints. What a refreshing joy it is to travel in any direction from the city through the lands of the Nez Perce tribe, known for breeding spotted Appaloosa horses, to admire cloud-covered mountainscapes and golden wheat fields that flow without boundaries; and at the end of the day, to eat meat and potatoes.

One fine place to get an archetypal Idaho meal is the Wolf Lodge Inn, at the eastern edge of Coeur d'Alene in an area known to naturalists for the bald eagles that congregate at the Mineral Ridge trail and on Beauty Bay in late autumn. A vast red barn-board roadhouse, just yards from the highway, this wild-west domain features oilcloth-clad tables and walls festooned with trophy animal heads, bleached bovine skulls, antique tools, old beer posters, vintage snowshoes, silly backwoods homilies, and yellowing newspaper clippings of local-interest stories. At the back of the rearmost dining area is a stone barbecue pit where tamarack and cherry wood burn a few feet below the grate. On this grate sizzle slabs of sirloin and filet mignon and porterhouses well over two pounds. The steaks are served with excellent steak fries, each of which is one-eighth of a long Idaho baker that has been sliced end to end and fried so that it develops a light, crisp skin and a creamy inside.

That fine meal was the inspiration for Chili Coeur d'Alene, which is rich in potatoes and stewlike in its heartiness. The dab of smoke flavoring is included to help conjure up the cozy perfume of woodburning stoves that hovers over so many local homes in the winter.

6 dried California chiles

3 tablespoons Snowcap lard

$^{1}/_{2}$ cup chopped red onion

2 scallions, chopped

2 garlic cloves, minced

1 pound boneless sirloin steak, trimmed of excess fat and cut into $^{1}/_{2}$-inch pieces

1 tablespoon chili powder

1 tablespoon sugar

2 teaspoons salt

$^{1}/_{2}$ tablespoon dried oregano

1 teaspoon freshly ground black pepper

1 teaspoon liquid smoke

2 tablespoons Worcestershire sauce

Two 10-ounce cans Ro-tel diced tomatoes and green chiles

3 large red-skinned potatoes, scrubbed and cut into $^{3}/_{4}$-inch pieces

3 large Yukon Gold potatoes, scrubbed and cut into $^{3}/_{4}$-inch pieces

1 tablespoon masa harina dissolved in $^{1}/_{4}$ cup warm water

1) Place the chiles in a large heatproof bowl and cover with boiling water. Let stand 30 minutes, until soft; then seed and stem them. In a food processor or blender, puree the chiles with 1 cup water. Set aside.

2) Heat the lard in a Dutch oven. Cook the onion, scallions, and garlic until soft. Add the steak and cook until browned. Drain off the excess fat. Add the chile puree, chili powder, sugar, salt, oregano, pepper, liquid smoke, Worcestershire sauce, and tomatoes. Bring to a boil; reduce the heat to a slow simmer and cook, partially covered, for 30 minutes. Add 1 cup of water and the potatoes. Stir well and cook, partially covered, 30 minutes more. Check the chili after 20 minutes; if it is getting too thick, add $^{1}/_{2}$ cup more water. Remove from the heat and add the masa harina mixture. Cook 5 minutes more.

Chicagoland
Chili Mac

THE COMBINATION OF CHILI-SEASONED ground beef, pasta, and beans is popular throughout the Midwest. In Cincinnati, it's layered and the noodles are spaghetti. To the west, around Lake Michigan, you are more likely to encounter chili in which all the ingredients are mixed together on the stove and the pasta is elbow macaroni. The latter is known as chili mac, which for many years was a staple in neighborhood taverns, diners, and town cafés around Chicagoland.

There is less chili mac on quick-eats menus in recent years—nachos and wings are the preferred bar food these days—but on a cold winter's day at home, when settling down for an afternoon of reading, TV viewing, or just hanging around the house, nothing induces a feeling of security and comfort better than the come-hither aroma of an honest pot of chili mac keeping warm on the stove.

1 pound lean ground chuck

2 tablespoons vegetable oil

One 28-ounce can diced tomatoes with juice

1 cup chopped onions

3 garlic cloves, minced

1 teaspoon salt

1 tablespoon Worcestershire sauce

2 tablespoons chili powder

1 teaspoon ground cumin

1 teaspoon dried marjoram

$^1/_2$ teaspoon freshly ground black pepper

2 tablespoons sugar

1 bay leaf

1 to 2 cups tomato sauce

Two 15$^1/_2$-ounce cans red kidney beans, drained and rinsed

Tabasco or other brand hot sauce

1 pound elbow macaroni

2 tablespoons butter

Grated cheese, optional

Oyster crackers, for garnish

1) Brown the beef in the oil in a Dutch oven, stirring to separate it. Drain the excess fat. Add the tomatoes, onions, garlic, salt, Worcestershire, chili powder, cumin, marjoram, pepper, sugar, bay leaf, and 1 cup of the tomato sauce. Partially cover and simmer 25 minutes, stirring occasionally, and adding additional tomato sauce to keep the chili nice and moist but not too soupy. Add the kidney beans and red pepper sauce. Cook 10 minutes more as you prepare the macaroni.

2) Cook the noodles until just tender. Drain and toss with the butter. Combine the hot noodles with the chili and serve in bowls, topped with grated cheese, if desired, and oyster crackers on the side.

Sunday Supper Chicken Chili

DINNER IN CENTRAL INDIANA MORE than likely means *chicken* dinner—a farmland favorite at home as well as in restaurants. On Sundays after church, and for supper any day of the week, chicken is a star on Hoosier tables.

This Indiana chili takes its cue from the state's great chicken dinners. It is a gentle, easy-to-eat fricassee with a country vegetable savor.

One 2¹/₂- to 3-pound chicken, quartered, with the skin

¹/₄ cup corn oil

1 cup chopped onions

1 cup chopped celery

Two 14¹/₂-ounce cans Ro-Tel diced tomatoes and chiles, with juice

One 14¹/₂-ounce can chicken broth

¹/₄ cup chili powder

1 tablespoon ground cumin

2 teaspoons dried Mexican oregano

1 teaspoon dried marjoram

1¹/₂ teaspoons salt

2 cups finely chopped red potatoes, with skin

1 cup finely chopped carrots

2 tablespoons masa harina dissolved in ¹/₂ cup of warm water

1) Wash the chicken parts and pat them dry. Heat the oil in a Dutch oven and set the chicken in it, skin side down. Cook 10 to 15 minutes, turning frequently, until browned. Remove the chicken from the Dutch oven and set aside.

2) Lower the heat and add the onions and celery to the pot; sauté until soft, using a spatula to scrape up the stuck chicken bits from the pan bottom. Add the tomatoes and broth along with the chili powder, cumin, oregano, marjoram, and salt. Simmer 10 minutes. Add the potatoes and carrots.

3) Return the chicken pieces to the pot. Cover and simmer 40 to 45 minutes, until the chicken is very tender. Turn the chicken and move the vegetables around in the pot several times as they cook. Remove the chicken from the pot; and when it is cool enough to handle, remove the skin and pull the meat from the bone in large shreds. Discard the skin and bones.

4) Add the masa harina mixture to the chili; mix well. Simmer until the chili begins to thicken. Return the shredded chicken to the Dutch oven; cook 10 minutes more.

Tall Corn
Pork Chili

IOWA

I N THE WAKE OF *THE BRIDGES OF MADI-son County,* Iowa's western farmlands now inspire millions of people to think of romance. We still think of pigs. No state in the union is more passionate about its pork (one out of sixteen jobs in the state is pig related), and there is no better place to eat a huge pork chop accompanied by a half-dozen fresh-picked ears of corn.

We've spent a lot of happy times in Iowa, partly for its natural beauty, much of which remains pretty much the way Grant Wood painted it, but mostly for its glorious farm food, which, beyond pork and corn, includes blue ribbon pies and cinnamon buns as big as a bulldog's head.

This recipe yields a satisfying bowl of gently spiced chili that reminds us of harvest time.

3/4 cup chopped onions

1 clove minced garlic

2 tablespoons corn oil

2 pounds boneless pork, trimmed of fat, cut into 1/2-inch cubes

1 tablespoon salt

1/2 teaspoon celery salt

1 teaspoon dried Mexican oregano

1 tablespoon sugar

4 tablespoons chili powder

1/2 tablespoon green jalapeño powder

One 14-ounce can chicken broth

One 15-ounce can tomato sauce

One 4 1/2-ounce can chopped green chiles, drained

Two 16-ounce cans corn, drained

1 tablespoon masa harina dissolved in 1/4 cup water

In a Dutch oven, cook the onions and garlic in the oil until soft. Add the pork. Cook until browned; then remove the pot from the heat. Add the salt, celery salt, oregano, sugar, chili powder, and jalapeño powder; stir well. Add the broth, 1 1/2 cups water, tomato sauce, and chiles. Return to the heat, bring to a boil, and then reduce the heat to a slow simmering boil. Cook, partially covered, for 1 hour. Add the corn and cook 15 minutes more. Add the masa harina mixture; cook 5 minutes more.

Porubsky's Grocery Store Chili

KANSAS

CHARLIE PORUBSKY'S CHILI HAS BEEN a lure to north Topeka since his mother started making it in the back of the family grocery store in 1951. Charlie learned to make it from his mother, and now his grown-up kids carry on the tradition—brewing up a few dozen gallons on an old four-burner stove behind the meat counter every morning for the lunchtime crowd. Porubsky's is still a neighborhood grocery store, and the dining area is just a small enclave off to one side, meaning the place gets mighty crowded every day starting at about 11 A.M. No chili is made on Fridays to keep the aisles clear for locals to do their shopping.

Porubsky's chili is midwestern style, meaning it is made with ground beef, it contains beans, and it is mildly spiced. Not one of the Porubsky family was able to write down the recipe for us for the simple reason that there is no recipe. It is a dish made by taste, feel, and experience: a little of this, a jot of that, a dash more of something else. We did spend a morning watching Charlie Jr. prepare a day's worth, so here is our educated version of Porubsky's pride. Its heat level can be adjusted by using hot or mild chili powder and by adding more or less hot sauce.

Porubsky's connoisseurs crumble a handful of saltines atop the bowl and garnish it with a scattering of hot horseradish-flavored pickle chips, which are also a Porubsky-made specialty.

FOR THE CHILI

1 cup chopped onions

2 garlic cloves, minced

2 tablespoons vegetable oil

2 pounds coarsely ground chuck

1 $^1/_2$ teaspoons salt

3 tablespoons chili powder

1 tablespoon ground cumin

2 teaspoons Worcestershire sauce

1 tablespoon sugar

3 cups tomato sauce

Two 16-ounce cans red kidney beans, drained

Tabasco to taste (we use 10 drops for a faint heat)

Saltine crackers

FOR HORSERADISH PICKLES

One 32-ounce jar kosher dill pickle halves (about 4 large pickles), with brine

$^1/_2$ cup prepared horseradish

1 teaspoon cayenne

Make the chili

In a big, heavy skillet or Dutch oven, sauté the onions and garlic in the oil until they are soft. Add the beef and salt. Cook until the beef is completely browned, breaking it up with a fork as it cooks. Drain off any excess fat. Add the chili powder, cumin, Worcestershire, sugar, tomato sauce, and 2 cups water. Bring the chili to a low boil and simmer 30 minutes, stirring occasionally. Add the beans and simmer 15 minutes more. Add the Tabasco and more salt, if desired.

Make the pickles

1) Pour the brine from the pickle jar into a large bowl. Mix the horseradish and cayenne into the brine. Cut the pickles into large bite-sized pieces and reimmerse them in the spiced brine. Cover and refrigerate several hours or overnight.

2) Serve the chili with saltines crumbled on top of each portion and garnish with pickle pieces.

Bluegrass
Burgoo Chili

BURGOO IS TO KENTUCKY COOKS WHAT barbecue is to Memphis pitmasters and martinis to mixologists: an opportunity for endless discussion, debate, and posturing in regard to the exact right way to make and serve it. A half a century ago when Cora, Rose, and Bob Brown wrote *America Cooks,* they quoted a man identified as "The Burgoo Master" of Louisville, who said the recipe required several fifty-gallon cauldrons, a butchered beef, a hog, and a lamb, as well as a few dozen freshly killed squirrels; and he said it should be served "always outdoors under the spreading shade of oak, elm, and ash—and always it should be preceded by libations drunk from frosted goblets of that drink for which Kentucky is also famous, the mint julep, with mint freshly gathered from the spring-house brook."

Still popular in the Bluegrass State at church suppers and as a party dish on or before Derby Day, burgoo is alleged to have gotten its name (pronounced *BUR-goo*) when a Civil War cook with a speech impediment tried to call the troops to a supper of "bird stew," but couldn't quite pronounce it right. Today's best burgoo is made year-round in the western part of the state in the vicinity of Owensboro, where (at least in restaurants) the game birds, opossums, and squirrels have been replaced by the local pitmaster's favorite barbecue meat, mutton. Burgoo tends to be hot and spicy, and it's still a mulligan stew, with several kinds of meats and vegetables; in other words, it makes a great bowl of chili!

Most recipes require at least a whole day of preparation (not including bagging and dressing the game) and hours of simmering, and they make enough to feed dozens of people. *Pace,* Kentucky burgoo chefs, but this one is nearly instant and serves a mere 8 to 10 people. It doubles easily if you're having a party (and big enough cauldrons in which to cook it).

4 dried chipotle chiles

2 dried ancho chiles

1 cup tomato sauce

$^1/_2$ cup diced onion

1 cup diced celery

4 garlic cloves, minced

2 tablespoons vegetable oil

Two 14$^1/_2$-ounce cans diced tomatoes with juice

One 10-ounce package frozen corn, defrosted

One 10-ounce package frozen lima beans, thawed

One 10-ounce package frozen okra, defrosted

$^2/_3$ pound pork sausage, cooked and cut into bite-size slices

$^2/_3$ pound white and dark cooked chicken meat, torn into shreds

$^2/_3$ pound cubed cooked lamb

2 teaspoons ground cumin

1 teaspoon freshly ground black pepper

2 teaspoons salt

1 to 2 cups barbecue sauce

Cooked rice

1) Place the chiles in a large heatproof bowl and cover with boiling water. Let stand 30 minutes, until soft; then seed and stem them. In a food processor, puree the chiles with the tomato sauce. Set aside.

2) In a Dutch oven, sauté the onion, celery, and garlic in the oil. Add the tomatoes, corn, lima beans, okra, and chile puree; stir in the meats and seasonings. Stir and simmer 25 to 30 minutes. As the chili simmers, add only enough barbecue sauce to keep it moist. The okra will help bind it, and this chili should be stew thick.

3) Serve on rice on the side.

Mardi Gras Vegetable Chili

LOUISIANA

W HEN WE INVITED OUR OLD FRIEND
Victor to dinner, he told us he had become a
vegetarian. Oh-oh! Victor is from New Orleans, and like most Cres-
cent City sons, he is a great eater and food lover who appreciates big
flavors and wild spices. We needed to serve him food as bold and colorful as a Fat Tuesday *fais-do-do*.

So we consulted one of our favorite community cookbooks, *River
Road Recipes,* a storehouse of Creole kitchen wizardry that has sold
over a million copies since the Junior League of Baton Rouge first published it in 1959. There we found a recipe for robust vegetable chili,
which became the basis of the meal we served Victor and have contin-
ued to enjoy even when nonvegetarians come for supper. If you are
antivegetarian as a matter of principle, it would be a fine idea to grill a
length of boudin sausage, cut it into 1-inch pieces, and add it to this
spicy brew.

6 large dried California chiles

4 cups canned vegetable broth

1 large eggplant, peeled and cut into 1-inch cubes

3 tablespoons olive oil

2 1/2 teaspoons salt

1 cup chopped onions

4 garlic cloves, minced

1 large red bell pepper, chopped

1/4 cup vegetable oil

2 teaspoons ground cumin

1 teaspoon ground allspice

2 teaspoons dried Mexican oregano

1 teaspoon freshly ground black pepper

1/2 tablespoon red jalapeño powder

One 14 1/2-ounce can Hunt's diced tomatoes with roasted garlic

One 15-ounce can golden hominy, drained

One 15-ounce can white kidney beans, drained

1 cup chopped fresh parsley

1 1/2 tablespoons sugar

1 tablespoon masa harina dissolved in 1/2 cup warm water

1) Place the chiles in a large heatproof bowl and cover with boiling water. Let stand 30 minutes, until soft; then seed and stem them. In a food processor or a blender, puree the chiles with 2 cups of the broth. Set aside.

2) Preheat the oven to 350°F. Coat the eggplant with the oil and place in a single layer in a 14 × 11-inch baking pan. Sprinkle it with 2 teaspoons of the salt. Bake about 30 minutes, until tender. Remove from the oven and set aside.

3) In a Dutch oven, sauté the onions, garlic, and bell pepper in the vegetable oil. When the vegetables are soft, add the chile puree and cooked eggplant along with the cumin, allspice, oregano, black pepper, the remaining $^1/_2$ teaspoon of salt, the jalapeño powder, tomatoes, hominy, beans, parsley, sugar, and the remaining 2 cups of broth. Cook over low heat at a simmering boil for 15 minutes. Add the masa harina mixture, and cook for 2 minutes more.

American
Chop Suey Chili

UNLESS YOU WENT TO CAMP OR BOARD-
ing school in Maine half a century ago or are a
connoisseur of arcane roadside culinaria, you might never have sam-
pled the strange New England dish known as American chop suey.
When we started traveling in the 1970s, it was still a common lunchtime
special on menus of small town cafés and antique diners away from the
lobster-centric restaurants of the Maine coast. You'll still find it served
at venerable Moody's of Waldoboro and Cole Farms of Grey, but its
thrifty nature runs completely contrary to food fashion.

What is particularly strange about American chop suey is that it
bears no resemblance to Chinese restaurant chop suey, except that it is
composed of lots of little chopped-up ingredients. How it got its Asian
name is lost in the mists of kitchen history, but one can surmise that it
was a penurious Yankee housewife or diner chef who figured out that

you could stretch a small amount of ground beef to feed a large number of people by adding macaroni and tomatoes. As opposed to slumgullion, cannibal stew, and such traditional frugal-sounding names for higgledy-piggledy meals, the title *American chop suey* gives them an exotic flavor.

Whatever its historical provenance, American chop suey was born to be made into a good Down East chili. True to the stolid nature of inland cookery, this transcendent Sloppy Joe is a gentle sort of chili, no fuss to make, and as easy on the palate as on the pocketbook.

NOTE: This recipe makes enough to serve four, six only if you're really stingy.

2 tablespoons vegetable oil

²/₃ cup chopped onions

1 cup diced celery (about 2 ribs)

1 pound lean ground chuck

Two 10-ounce cans Ro-tel diced tomatoes and green chiles

1 teaspoon ground cumin

1 tablespoon chili powder

1 teaspoon salt

8 ounces elbow macaroni

1 cup grated sharp Cheddar cheese

Chow mein noodles, for garnish

1) Heat the oil in a heavy saucepan and sauté the onions and celery until soft. Stir in the ground beef and cook until browned, breaking it into a pebbly consistency. Drain the excess fat. Add the tomatoes and green chiles, cumin, chili powder, and salt. Simmer vigorously 15 minutes or so to reduce the liquid.

2) As the chili simmers, cook the elbow macaroni until tender. Drain. Stir the macaroni into the beef mixture.

3) Divide into 4 bowls and serve the chili piping hot with the cheese melting on top. Sprinkle on the chow mein noodles as a garnish.

Chesapeake Bay Chili
MARYLAND

ALTHOUGH BALTIMORE IS BEST KNOWN for hot-spiced crabs, it is also a city that once prided itself on the creamiest seafood stews between Boston and Savannah. We're thinking in particular of the old, long-departed Chesapeake House, where the finest seafood in town was served in high style by a staff of waiters with a tenure that probably went back to some time just after the Civil War.

In remembrance of such bygone silver chafing-dish meals and in salute to the rich crab imperial that is still a specialty of many local crab houses, this seafood chili is as mild as chili can be: svelte and ineffably deluxe, with only enough pepper to keep the tastebuds from falling into a happy, cream-induced stupor. It is a very unusual chili, but one of our favorites when comfort food is required.

2 tablespoons butter

$^1/_4$ cup chopped
scallions

1 cup chopped celery

1 pound medium shrimp,
peeled

1 cup heavy cream

$^1/_2$ cup whole milk

1 $^1/_2$ tablespoons all-
purpose flour

1 teaspoon salt

1 teaspoon ground white
pepper

1 teaspoon celery salt

$^1/_2$ tablespoon chili
powder

1 pound fresh crabmeat,
picked over to remove
any bits of shell or
cartilage (the better the
crab, the better this dish
will taste)

2 eggs, hard cooked and
sliced

Cooked rice

1) In a heavy skillet or saucepan, melt the butter
and sauté the scallions and celery until soft. Add
the shrimp and sauté until pink.

2) In a small bowl, combine the cream and milk
and stir in the flour until smooth. Add the cream
mixture to the skillet along with the salt, pepper,
celery salt, and chili powder. Stir and cook over
low heat until the mixture thickens. Gently stir in
the crabmeat and eggs.

3) Serve at once; this chili does not improve with
age. Serve on white rice.

Rock-Ribbed
Bean-and-Beef Chili
MASSACHUSETTS

NEW ENGLANDERS TEND TO BE CULINARILY dowdy and proud of it. Yankee cuisine is one of thrift and forthright flavors, characterized by duffs, pandowdies, chowders, stews, and a prominent bean pot. In such a spirit, we invented an honest chili with no pyrotechnical frills, but with plenty of good indigenous beans. It is not a fiery kind of chili—Down Easters don't like to get their blood aboil for nothing—but it has just the right warming effect on a cold winter's afternoon. There is nothing in this recipe that isn't readily available at any sensible grocery store. We like Peddler's Savory Soup Sack made in Southbury, Connecticut. It contains great northern, pinto, red, kidney, and navy beans, although if you do use this product, omit the seasoning pack and the few bits of pasta included. Goya also puts out a good bean mix.

One 12-ounce package of mixed dried beans.

^{1}/2 cup chopped onion

2 garlic cloves, minced

2 tablespoons vegetable oil

1 ^{1}/2 pounds ground chuck

One 28-ounce can crushed tomatoes

2 tablespoons molasses

1 tablespoon packed brown sugar

2 tablespoons mild chili powder

1 tablespoon salt

1 cup shredded Cheddar cheese

1) Soak the beans overnight. Drain and add fresh water to cover. Bring the beans to a boil and simmer for 1 hour, until tender, skimming foam from the pot. Or place the dried beans in large pot, cover with water, and bring to a boil. Boil 1 or 2 minutes. Cover, remove from the heat, and let stand 1 hour. Return the beans to the heat and cook 2 hours, until tender. Set aside.

2) In large skillet or Dutch oven, cook the onion and garlic in the oil until soft. Add the beef and brown it, stirring to separate the meat so it is crumbly. Drain off the excess fat. Add the tomatoes, molasses, brown sugar, chili powder, and salt. Cook 20 minutes, uncovered, stirring occasionally. Drain the beans and add to the meat mixture. Cook a few minutes to reheat.

3) Serve the chili topped with the cheese. A slice of steamed brown bread on the side is a nice touch.

Cornish Miner
Chili Pasties

PASTIES ARE THE LOCAL SPECIALTY OF Michigan's U.P. (Upper Peninsula), where Cornish miners used to take them to work and heat them for lunch on the end of a shovel. Made of beef (or beef and pork) and vegetables inside a sturdy pastry crust, they were a hearty, portable meal.

Today when you travel from Sault Ste. Marie to Ishpeming and from Ironwood to Copper Harbor, you'll encounter all manner of pasties—some portable and tidy, some covered with gravy and edible only with a knife and fork. Many restaurants offer their own twist on the traditional ingredients—gourmet pasties filled with steak, pizza pasties with pepperoni and mozzarella inside, even vegetarian pasties for meat-phobes. Being such a flexible character, the pasty is a natural repository for a stout, beefy chili, although chili's tendency toward soupiness precludes portability. Our recipe is a hearty one, but surprisingly low in fat and high in vegetable consciousness.

We find that a microwave oven makes this recipe a breeze. The diced potatoes, carrots, and turnips can each be zapped in the micro-wave, a few minutes per vegetable, until they are just tender, requiring only a few more minutes of cooking, which they'll have in the fry pan with the beef and in the oven, baking inside the crust.

Also, although it is possible to make your own dough—a rugged pie crust is what you want—we're perfectly content to streamline things by using ready-made pie crusts, found in the refrigerator case at the supermarket.

NOTE: This recipe makes pasties for 4.

1 cup diced onions

1 tablespoon butter plus 2 tablespoons melted

$^3/_4$ pound sirloin steak, trimmed of fat and cut into $^1/_4$-inch pieces

$^2/_3$ cup tomato sauce

1 $^1/_2$ cups diced red-skinned potatoes, skin on, lightly cooked (6 to 7 minutes in the microwave)

1 cup diced carrots, lightly cooked (3 to 4 minutes in the microwave)

1 cup diced turnips, lightly cooked (3 to 4 minutes in the microwave)

One 4$^1/_2$-ounce can chopped green chiles, drained

1 tablespoon chili powder

1 teaspoon ground cumin

1 tablespoon chopped fresh marjoram

1 teaspoon salt

$^1/_2$ teaspoon hot red pepper flakes

2 packages refrigerated pie crusts (4 crusts total)

1) Preheat the oven to 400°F. Lightly grease two cookie sheets.

2) In a large, heavy skillet over medium heat, sauté the onion in 1 tablespoon of the butter until soft. Add the beef and cook until lightly browned. Drain off any excess fat. Add all the remaining ingredients, except the pie crusts and melted butter. Sauté 10 minutes and remove from the heat. Allow the chili filling to cool to near room temperature.

3) Unfold the pie crusts. Place one-quarter of the filling in the middle of each crust. Fold each crust in half and crimp firmly with a fork to create a half-circle. Paint the crusts lightly with the melted butter. Use a spatula to lift each pasty onto the prepared cookie sheets. Bake 15 minutes, until light golden brown.

4) Use a spatula to lift the pasties from the cookie sheets to plates. Be careful; if unsupported, they can break in two like tender hearts.

Café Brenda
Black Bean
Vegetable Chili

MINNESOTA

ALTHOUGH EVERYONE SHOULD START
the day in Minneapolis over plates of pancakes at
Al's diner and celebrate the sunset with highballs and "silver but-
terknife" beef steaks at Murray's, there is another, entirely different
sort of restaurant that food lovers who visit Minneapolis need to try.
It's called Café Brenda, and its proprietor, Brenda Langton, has been a
significant force in the health-food movement hereabouts since she
opened Café Kardamena in St. Paul more than twenty years ago. That's
right: health food! Even if you are devoted to red meat and high fat (as
we are with no apologies), this is one restaurant with brilliant flavors
and satisfying meals you don't want to miss!

"We think of our food as comforting and rejuvenating," Brenda
wrote in her introduction to *The Café Brenda Cookbook*. "It's food that
is nutritious, tastes good while you're eating it, and feels good hours

after you've eaten it." As proof of her words, we offer her recipe for delicious vegetable chili designed to please the fussiest nutrition wardens as well as hard-core chiliheads.

Brenda's black bean chili often appears on the lunch menu, served with a slab of rough-hewn corn bread on the side. Wild rice is a good Minnesota companion for this dish, too. Whatever else you serve, do not neglect the roasted pumpkin seeds to sprinkle on top: Their toasty crunch is addictive. As for the cheese and sour cream garnishes, we suggest them only for those who simply can't tolerate a chili as low in fat as this one is without them.

This recipe makes enough for 8 to 10 servings. Leftovers are a side dish that fits with everything from morning eggs to crown roast of pork. At Café Brenda, this chili is often used as a filling for enchiladas.

And note that the beans require a long soak before the chili is prepared . . . although in a pinch, the quick-soak method could be used (page 5).

2¹/₂ cups dried black beans

1 large onion, chopped

2 tablespoons olive oil

4 garlic cloves, minced

2 large carrots, diced

2 ribs celery, chopped

1 red bell pepper, seeded and chopped

2 to 3 jalapeño peppers, seeded and minced

1 tablespoon minced fresh marjoram or 1 teaspoon dried

1 tablespoon minced fresh oregano or 1 teaspoon dried Mexican

1 tablespoon chili powder

1 tablespoon ground cumin

¹/₂ teaspoon cayenne

¹/₂ teaspoon crushed coriander seeds

1¹/₂ teaspoons salt

Juice of ¹/₂ lemon

1 ounce unsweetened chocolate

1 cup raw pumpkin seeds

Soy sauce

Sour cream, optional

1¹/₂ cups grated Cheddar cheese, optional

1) Pick over the black beans, then soak them in 8 cups of water for 6 to 8 hours. Drain them and cook in 8 cups of water until tender, about 1 hour. Drain, reserving all the cooking liquid.

2) In a large skillet, sauté the onion in the oil until soft. Add the garlic, carrots, and celery; sauté 3 minutes. Add the bell pepper and jalapeño peppers; sauté 3 to 5 minutes longer.

3) Combine the sautéed vegetables and cooked beans in a large pot. Add the herbs, spices, salt, lemon juice, and chocolate. Pour in about 1¹/₂ cups of the reserved cooking liquid or as needed to keep the chili loose. Simmer 30 minutes, stirring occasionally.

4) As the chili simmers, place the pumpkin seeds in a sauté pan over medium-high heat. Dry-toast them, stirring and tossing until the seeds glisten and begin to brown. Sprinkle a few drops of soy sauce on them and allow them to cool.

5) Serve in bowls with the pumpkin seeds sprinkled on top. Add sour cream and/or grated cheese, if desired.

Highway 61 Chili

THROUGHOUT MUCH OF THE SOUTH, the meat of choice is pork; and one of the unheralded dishes often found on café menus is a kind of stew made from shredded barbecued pork and summer vegetables. As it is traditionally made in the region, pork stew is luscious, sweet, and mildly spiced. But we have found that east of Highway 61, as the old blues highway threads through the Mississippi River Delta, pork is often served with a hot, hot sauce that seems to be so paradoxically satisfying in the humid 100°F air.

This chili is inspired by fiery pork stews we remember from lunch counters in Clarksdale, Indianola, and Yazoo City. The hot chiles complement the sweet pork in a way that is succulent synergy; and the smoky taste of the chipotles makes this dish a kind of Mississippi magic.

4 dried chipotle chiles

2 dried ancho chiles

1 cup barbecue sauce

1 cup chopped onions

1 tablespoon butter

1 $^1/_3$ pounds ground pork

One 14 $^1/_2$-ounce can diced tomatoes, drained

One 15 $^1/_2$-ounce can corn niblets, drained

1 tablespoon Worcestershire sauce

Up to 1 cup tomato sauce

Cornbread

1) Place the chiles in a large heatproof bowl and cover with boiling water. Let stand 30 minutes, until soft; then seed and stem them. In a food processor or blender, puree the chiles with the barbecue sauce. Set aside.

2) In a heavy skillet or Dutch oven, sauté the onions in the butter until soft. Add the pork and cook and stir until the meat is cooked thoroughly. Drain the excess fat. Add the chile puree, tomatoes, corn, and Worcestershire sauce. Cook and stir 10 minutes, adding up to 1 cup of tomato sauce to keep the chili moist.

3) Serve with corn bread.

Mule-Kicking Hot Chili

MISSOURI HAS MANY CLAIMS TO CULI-
nary fame, from the barbecue and fried chicken
of Kansas City to the snoot (fried pig snout!) sandwiches and toasted
ravioli of St. Louis. It is also the home of Anheuser-Busch, which gives
us the opportunity to brew up a recipe in which good ol' Budweiser
plays a featured role. The other inspiration for this suds-based bowl of
fire-and-spice is the good sausage found in butcher shops all over St.
Louis.

3 dried ancho chiles

2 dried pasilla chiles

2 dried chipotle chiles

$^1/_2$ cup chopped onion

2 garlic cloves, minced

2 tablespoons vegetable oil

1 pound beef round, trimmed of fat and cut into $^1/_2$-inch cubes

$1^1/_2$ pounds sweet Italian sausage

1 tablespoon sugar

1 teaspoon salt

1 teaspoon freshly ground black pepper

1 teaspoon dried Mexican oregano

$1^1/_2$ teaspoons prepared hot mustard

1 can Budweiser beer, or your choice of non-yuppie brew

1 tablespoon masa harina dissolved in $^1/_4$ cup warm water

1) Place the chiles in a large heatproof bowl and cover with boiling water. Let stand 30 minutes, until soft; stem and seed them. In a food processor or blender, puree the chiles with the water. Set aside.

2) In a Dutch oven, sauté the onion and garlic in the oil until soft. Add the beef and cook it until browned. Drain the excess fat. Set aside.

3) Preheat the broiler or grill. Cook the sausages under the broiler or on the grill until they are cooked through and crisp skinned. Cut into 1-inch discs and add to the Dutch oven along with the chile puree, sugar, salt, pepper, oregano, mustard, and beer. Stir well and bring to a boil. Reduce the heat and cook at a simmering boil, partially covered, for 40 minutes. Add the masa harina mixture and cook for 10 more minutes.

Working Person's Green Chili Bowl

LAST TIME WE VISITED BILLINGS, THE town was abuzz about Robert Redford's movie *The Horse Whisperer*. Much of it was filmed around Big Timber, not far away, and Billings' premier saddle maker, Chas Weldon, had supplied the saddles, tack, and chaps. We spent a morning with Chas, talking "Beef, Beans, and B.S." (the name of a cowboy roundup he hosts annually) and hearing about his adventures outfitting Redford and the cast.

Our eyes filled with stardust, we left his shop and headed for El Burrito, a tiny storefront cafeteria about as far from Hollywood glamour as any place could be. Honestly, we don't know if Redford ever dined here, but if the moviemakers were looking for a slice of real life in modern Montana, this is it. Prices are low (under $5 for a good meal), and everybody totes his or her own disposable plate of food from the kitchen window to a table. Atop the menu, El Burrito boasts that it is "The Working Person's Eating Place."

You can get chili for breakfast in the form of *huevos rancheros,* at lunch atop smothered burritos, and at dinner as a main course in one of two variations: red chili, made with beef, and green chili, made with pork. True to the pure palates of those who consider chili nearly sacred, beans are presented only on the side (in refried form), as are rice or potatoes and tortillas. We especially like the tortillas, which are so good for mopping the last drops of delicious soupy chili from the plate.

6 fresh long green (New Mexico) chiles

1 cup chicken broth

2 tablespoons vegetable oil

3 garlic cloves, minced

$^{1}/_{2}$ cup chopped onion

2 pounds boneless pork tenderloin, cut into $^{1}/_{4}$-inch pieces

1 teaspoon crushed dried tarragon

1 teaspoon dried sage

1 tablespoon green jalapeño powder

1 teaspoon ground cumin

1 teaspoon salt

1) Preheat the broiler. Prepare the chiles by placing them under the broiler and turning them carefully until they are charred all over. Wrap them in wet paper towels; and when cool enough to handle, skin and seed them. Place the chiles' flesh in a blender with the broth. Puree and set aside.

2) Heat the oil in a large, heavy skillet. Add the garlic and onion and sauté until soft. Add the pork; cook and stir until well browned. Add the chile puree and the remaining ingredients. Stir well. Bring to a simmer over low heat and cook 8 to 10 minutes.

Church Supper
Chili Mac and Cheese
NEBRASKA

T WAS AT A HELP-YOURSELF CHURCH SUP-
per buffet west of Broken Bow many years ago that we
came across this endearing chili variation, which we have always asso-
ciated with the straightforward farm cooking of Nebraska. At first, we
assumed it was two separate things to eat. But the lady ahead of us in
line, recognizing we were strangers to the town and to the townsfolk's
cooking, told us that the two casserole dishes—one filled with classic
macaroni and cheese, the other with a meaty chili—were her neigh-
bor's contribution to supper every week, without fail. Then she showed
us that the proper way to put them on the plate was to lay out a bed of
macaroni and then pile a scoop of meaty chili on top. An excellent combination!

We confess that sometimes, when feeling lazy or in need of the
corporate kind of comfort that boxed meals provide, we don't bother to

make our macaroni and cheese from scratch, but rather just brew up a batch of boxed Kraft Dinner (and make it a little less soupy than the official recipe calls for). But here's the full-scale way to do it, yielding a dish anyone would be proud to bring to a church supper.

FOR THE MACARONI AND CHEESE

12 ounces elbow macaroni

3 tablespoons butter

3 tablespoons all-purpose flour

1 cup milk

1 teaspoon salt

1 teaspoon dry mustard

2 cups grated Cheddar cheese

FOR THE CHILI

1 cup chopped onions

2 garlic cloves, minced

2 tablespoons vegetable oil

1 pound ground chuck

1 cup barbecue sauce

2 tablespoons chili powder

1 teaspoon ground cumin

1 teaspoon salt

$^1/_2$ teaspoon freshly ground black pepper

2 teaspoons Worcestershire sauce

Up to 1 cup crushed tomatoes

Make the macaroni and cheese

1) Bring a large pot of water to boil. Add salt and cook macaroni 5 to 8 minutes, until just tender. Drain.

2) Preheat the oven to 350°F. Butter a $2^1/_2$- to 3-quart casserole.

3) Melt the butter in a heavy-bottomed saucepan. Sprinkle in the flour, stirring constantly. Heat the milk to just below boiling and stir it into the flour-butter mixture, stirring constantly until thickened. Add the salt and mustard.

4) In a large bowl, combine the macaroni, white sauce, and cheese, stirring just enough to blend it. Pour the mixture into the casserole and bake for 30 minutes.

Make the chili

1) In a heavy skillet, sauté the onions and garlic in the oil until soft. Add the beef and cook until browned, breaking up any clumps. Drain any excess fat. Add the barbecue sauce, chili powder, cumin, salt, pepper, and Worcestershire sauce. Simmer for 15 minutes. Add as much crushed tomatoes as needed to keep the chili loose.

2) Serve the chili in broad, shallow bowls atop the macaroni and cheese.

Cowboy Poetry Chili

ELKO, NEVADA, IS AN OLD COW TOWN to which sheepherders historically repaired from the western slopes to find shelter for the coldest part of the year and wait for the spring thaw. While in town, it was their custom to stay in hotels that featured big Basque feasts served at communal dinner tables. These days, Elko is host to the annual Cowboy Poetry and Music Gatherings, to which real buckaroos and cowboy wanna-bes from all over the West (and East) come each January and June to recite and listen to tales of life on the range.

At the close of day, after the singing workshops are done and before the bars and casinos start to fill up, buckaroo bards in Stetsons and Justin boots flock to the dinner halls on Silver Street to dine on huge meals of classic Basque food. Our Cowboy Poetry Chili was inspired by these rip-snortin' Basque meals and is tasty enough to make even the most frog-voiced (like us) want to sing.

2 tablespoons olive oil

10 garlic cloves, minced

2 pounds ground lamb

One 28-ounce can tomatillos, drained

2 teaspoons ground cumin

1 1/2 teaspoons green jalapeño powder

2 tablespoons chili powder

1/2 cup chopped fresh cilantro or 1 tablespoon dried

2 tablespoons sugar

1 tablespoon salt

Juice of 1 lemon

1/2 cup chopped fresh parsley

One 15 1/2-ounce can pink beans, drained

2 tablespoons masa harina dissolved in 1/2 cup warm water

1/2 loaf of store-bought or homemade garlic bread, cut into 1-inch cubes

1) Heat the oil in a Dutch oven and add the garlic; cook until soft. Add the lamb and cook until browned. Drain off any excess fat.

2) In a food processor or blender, puree the tomatillos. Add to the Dutch oven along with the cumin, jalapeño powder, chili powder, cilantro, sugar, salt, lemon juice, parsley, and 2 cups water. Bring to a boil; cook at a slow boil for 30 minutes, partially covered. Add the beans and cook 10 minutes more. Add the masa harina mixture and cook 7 minutes more. Remove from the heat.

3) This chili is on the soupy side even when bound with the masa harina. It is best served in soup bowls and topped with crusty cubes of garlic bread that can be used to sop up the good juices.

Yankee Bean Pot Chili

FOR AS LONG AS WE HAVE BEEN MARRIED, a pillar on our regional cookbook shelf has been *The New England Yankee Cookbook*, written by Imogene Wolcott in 1939. Featuring not only regional recipes and lore, it also includes antique photos of local heroes: a clam digger in his rubber boots, a white-haired granny rolling out the dough for cookies, a stalwart family at its dinner table. Even better than the book itself is the fact that we found it in a secondhand store somewhere in New Hampshire and its previous owner had used it well. It is stained, blotched, and strewn with evidence of someone none-too-neat in the kitchen, who apparently tried nearly every recipe; and many of those recipes are annotated with the cook's comments.

Some twenty years ago when we saw an enthusiastic *Very Good!* written in pencil next to the New Hampshire Baked Yellow Eye Pork

and Beans recipe, we knew we should try it. We did, and with only minor modifications, it became our standard recipe for serious, stout-
flavored Yankee pork and beans. Add a good measure of pureed chiles
and it becomes a bowl of red with one heckuva punch—not exactly
vegetarian (the salt pork is essential) but not beefy either.

Although the recipe requires little effort, it does demand lots of
time for soaking the beans and cooking them *slowly*.

2¹/₂ cups dried yellow-eye beans

2 cups barbecue sauce

³/₄ cup packed brown sugar

¹/₂ cup molasses

1 tablespoon prepared yellow mustard

¹/₂ teaspoon freshly ground black pepper

1 teaspoon ground ginger

2 teaspoons salt

8 dried whole ancho chile peppers

³/₄ pound salt pork, scored deeply with a knife on the nonrind side

1) Wash the beans and soak overnight in cold water. Drain. Place the beans in a large pot and cover with fresh water. Simmer 60 to 90 minutes, until the skins start to wrinkle. Drain. In a large bowl, mix the beans with 1 cup of the barbecue sauce, the sugar, molasses, mustard, pepper, ginger, and salt.

2) Place the chiles in a large heatproof bowl and cover with boiling water. Let stand 30 minutes, until soft; then seed and stem them. In a food processor or blender, puree the chiles with the remaining 1 cup of barbecue sauce.

3) Preheat the oven to 300°F. Add the chile puree to the beans, mix, and turn into a bean pot. Place the salt pork on top of the beans with the rind side up. Cover the bean pot and bake for 5 hours. Uncover for the last hour so the beans get crusty.

Chili of the
Garden State

F ANYONE NEEDS PROOF OF NEW JERSEY'S
sobriquet, The Garden State, we recommend a summer-
time trip to Delicious Orchards in Colt's Neck. Here you'll find tomatoes still on the vine; corn picked that morning; and ultra-fresh peas,
beans, corn, etc., etc. We always come away with armloads of gorgeous
fruits and vegetables, a peach crumb pie or two, chocolate chip muffins
for the next morning, freshly made pound cakes for dessert, and
caramel-coated marshmallows for snacking.

This vegetarian chili, using three different kinds of tomatoes, was
inspired by the Delicious Orchards bounty. It's an easy recipe, requiring
little more than the assembly of ingredients—the fresher, the better.
Note that the jalapeño pepper is optional. Without it, this is a mild garden chili. With a jalapeño or two or a spoonful of the atomic-strength
jalapeño powder from Pendery's (page 9), it can be a four-alarmer.

1 1/2 cups chopped onions

1 1/2 cups chopped celery

3 tablespoons corn oil

1/2 cup diced carrots

1 red bell pepper, seeded and chopped

1 green bell pepper, seeded and chopped

6 garlic cloves, minced

2 1/2 to 3 1/2 cups crushed canned tomatoes

3 oil-packed sun-dried tomatoes, chopped (available in gourmet stores and most supermarkets)

1 teaspoon crushed red pepper flakes

2 teaspoons ground cumin

3 tablespoons chili powder

2 teaspoons dried Mexican oregano

1 teaspoon salt

1 to 2 finely minced jalapeño peppers or 1 to 2 teaspoons green jalapeño powder, optional

2 large ripe tomatoes, blanched, skinned, and chopped

2 cups corn kernels, fresh or frozen and thawed

One 15 1/2-ounce can white kidney beans, rinsed and drained

Grated Cheddar cheese

Sour cream

Saltine crackers

1) In a Dutch oven, sauté the onions and celery in the oil until soft. Add the carrots and bell pepper; cook until they begin to soften; then add the garlic. As the garlic softens, add 2 1/2 cups of the crushed tomatoes, the sun-dried tomatoes, red pepper flakes, cumin, chili powder, oregano, and salt. If you want this chili *hot*, add the jalapeño pepper. Simmer over low heat 20 minutes, stirring often, adding more crushed tomatoes, if necessary to keep the chili moist. Add the fresh tomatoes, corn, and beans. Simmer another 10 minutes.

2) Serve with the cheese strewn on top of individual bowls, and garnish with the sour cream and crackers.

Mesilla Valley
Bowl of Green

I F THE CULINARY SOUL OF TEXAS IS A bowl of red, then that of New Mexico is a bowl of green, also known as *chile verde*. New Mexico is *the* chile state, the only one we know to have declared chile its official state vegetable. (In truth, the state legislature, after debating the issue at some length, anointed *two* state vegetables—the chile and the pinto bean—and chile is, technically, a fruit . . . but that's another story.) From the growing fields of the Mesilla Valley in the south to the foothills of the Sangre de Cristo Mountains north of Santa Fe, colorful chile *ristras* (wreaths) are used to decorate homes and businesses; and rare is the restaurant that doesn't feature chili in some form on its breakfast, lunch, and/or dinner menu.

Nowhere is New Mexico's chile passion more intense than in the little town of Hatch, north of Las Cruces, where a huge chile festival is staged every year early in the autumn as the harvest begins. The whole town goes chile mad. Pretty girls vie for the titles of red and green chile queens (green is chile fresh from the vine; red is ripened) and other locals ride through town on parade floats dressed like pepper pods. Growers, pickers, and chile fans of every stripe turn out to eat and be merry. All along the side of the road, people set up roasters to cook fresh chiles and sell the soft, aromatic roasted pods by the bag to take home for cooking or for sandwiches to eat on the spot. It is the most fun a chilihead can have.

Our recipe for green chili is one we learned at the festival in Hatch. It is a celebration of the chile pepper with no distraction from beans, an elemental way to taste this unique vegetable's earthy character.

4 dried green chiles or 4 fresh New Mexico chile peppers

One 28-ounce can tomatillos, drained

2 pounds lean round steak, cut into $1/4$-inch cubes

$1/3$ cup all-purpose flour

$1/2$ cup lard

$1/4$ cup scallions cut into $1/2$-inch lengths

4 garlic cloves, minced

2 tablespoons vegetable oil

$1/2$ tablespoon dried Mexican oregano

$1/2$ tablespoon ground cumin

$1/2$ tablespoon sugar

$1 1/2$ tablespoons salt

One $14 1/2$-ounce can beef broth

1 cup fresh parsley, chopped

1 cup fresh cilantro, chopped

1 tablespoon masa harina dissolved in $1/4$ cup water

1) If using dried chiles, place them in a large heatproof bowl and cover with boiling water. Let stand 30 minutes, until soft; then seed and stem them. If using fresh chiles, roast, peel, and seed them. In a food processor or blender puree the chiles with 1 cup water until they are smooth and set aside.

2) Puree the tomatillos and set aside. (Do not puree the tomatillos and chiles together, because the chiles require more time in the food processor than do the tomatillos.)

3) Dredge the beef in the flour. In a large skillet, melt the lard. In manageable batches, fry the beef cubes until they are browned, removing them from the skillet to drain on paper towels.

4) In a Dutch oven, cook the scallions and garlic in the oil until soft. Add the beef, oregano, cumin, sugar, and salt. Add the broth and pureed chiles and tomatillos. Stir in the parsley and cilantro; bring to a boil. Reduce the heat to a low simmering boil and cook, partially covered, for 1 hour 10 minutes. Add the masa harina mixture to pot; stir and cook 10 minutes more.

Buffalo Beef and Weck Chili

THE PRE-EMINENT SANDWICH OF UPSTATE New York is Buffalo's beef on weck: The *weck* refers to an absorbent bulky roll dotted with kummelweck—caraway seeds. With a schmear of horseradish or hot mustard and enough natural beef gravy to soften the roll, it's well-nigh a perfect sandwich. Taverns and beef houses throughout the city make a specialty of it; and connoisseurs debate whose roast beef is more luxurious and where the kummelweck rolls are freshest.

Our New York chili is an ode to this great upstate sandwich. It is a dish at once peppery, sweet, and tart—all qualities that amplify the luxury of pillow-soft roast beef and make this chili sparkle on the tongue.

NOTE: This recipe makes 4 servings.

6 dried ancho chiles

2 to 2^1/$_2$ cups beef broth

1 cup broken gingersnap cookies

1 cup chopped onions

2 tablespoons vegetable oil

^{2}/$_3$ cup crushed canned tomatoes

1 tablespoon prepared yellow mustard

1 tablespoon prepared horseradish

^{1}/$_3$ cup packed dark brown sugar

1 teaspoon ground ginger

1^1/$_2$ teaspoons salt

2 tablespoons whole caraway seeds

1^1/$_2$ pounds thinly sliced cooked roast beef

8 slices seeded rye bread

1) Place the chiles in a heatproof bowl and cover with boiling water. Let stand 30 minutes, until soft; then seed and stem them. In a food processor or blender, puree the chiles with 1^1/$_2$ cups of the broth and the gingersnaps. Set aside.

2) In a heavy skillet, sauté the onions in the oil. Stir in the chile puree, tomatoes, mustard, horseradish, brown sugar, ginger, salt, and caraway seeds. Lower the heat and cook 10 minutes, adding up to 1 cup more broth, as needed to keep the mixture loose. Add the beef 1 minute before serving. (If added sooner, it will toughen.)

3) Serve on slices of seeded rye bread that is soft enough to absorb the juices.

Pig Chili

JUST AS TARHEELS LIKE THEIR BARBECUED meats to be basic, with sauce a mere note of flavor to accentuate the adoration of pure pork, so this North Carolina chili is simplicity itself: pork and pureed chiles, haloed by the distinctive vinegar tang local chefs use to bring out the flavor of their smokehouse viands. We use chipotles for their heat and smoky savor, and just enough red stuff to keep it moist.

2 pounds pork loin

4 dried chipotle chiles

2 dried ancho chiles

1 cup crushed tomatoes

$^{1}/_{2}$ cup chopped onion

$^{1}/_{4}$ cup vegetable oil

$^{1}/_{2}$ cup cider vinegar

1 teaspoon ground cumin

1 tablespoon Worcestershire sauce

1 tablespoon sugar

Hush puppies or corn bread

1) Preheat the oven to 350°F. Place the pork in a baking pan and roast 1 hour, until cooked through. When cool enough to handle, tear the meat into bite-sized shreds and set aside.

2) Place the chiles in a large heatproof bowl and cover with boiling water. Let stand 30 minutes, until soft; then seed and stem them. In a food processor or blender, puree the chiles with the tomatoes. Set aside.

3) In a large heavy skillet or Dutch oven, sauté the onion in the oil. When the onion begins to soften, add the shredded pork, tossing and stirring it in the hot oil. While tossing, drizzle in the vinegar. Add the chile puree, cumin, Worcestershire, and sugar. Lower the heat and simmer 5 minutes.

4) Serve with hush puppies or corn bread.

Forty Below
Meat Loaf and
Mashed Potatoes Chili

FOR LOVERS OF SQUARE MEALS, NORTH Dakota is a good place to travel. In small communities throughout the state you'll come across inconspicuous restaurants with soul-satisfying menus of meat and potatoes with blue-ribbon cream pie for dessert.

Not many travelers visit in the winter—we once saw a bumper sticker around Bismarck that said, "40 Below Keeps the Riff-Raff Out." But it was on a cold-weather pilgrimage to Strasburg—Lawrence Welk's hometown—that we stopped in a roadside restaurant many years ago and discovered what has become a favorite twist on the meat loaf and mashed potatoes theme: the "igloo meat loaf." It combines the meat and potatoes in a one-dish casserole. That meat loaf subsequently became the inspiration for this north country chili, which, unlike most chilies, is best eaten immediately—while the mashed potatoes on top are fresh and fluffy.

FOR THE CHILI

2 strips bacon

$1/4$ cup chopped onion

2 garlic cloves, minced

2 pounds mixed ground meat (equal parts pork, veal, and beef)

1 tablespoon dried Mexican oregano

$1/2$ tablespoon salt

1 teaspoon freshly ground black pepper

1 teaspoon onion powder

2 tablespoons chili powder

One 15-ounce can tomato sauce

2 tablespoons ketchup

1 tablespoon Kitchen Bouquet browning and seasoning sauce

1 tablespoon sugar

1 cup shredded Cheddar cheese

FOR THE MASHED POTATOES

6 medium Yukon Gold potatoes, peeled and halved

1 tablespoon butter

1 cup warm milk

2 tablespoons sour cream

$1/2$ tablespoon salt

Make the chili

1) In a Dutch oven, cook the bacon until crisp. Remove the bacon and set aside. In the remaining fat, cook the onion and garlic until they are soft. Add the ground meat. Brown well, stirring and mixing to break it up as it cooks. Drain any excess fat.

2) Crumble the bacon and add it to the meat. Stir in all the remaining ingredients, except the cheese. Add $1/2$ cup water, stir well, and bring to a boil. Reduce the heat to a slow simmer and cook, uncovered, 40 minutes, until the mixture is thick and not at all soupy. Preheat the oven to 200°F. Transfer the chili to a 2-quart casserole. Cover and place in the oven to keep warm.

Make the mashed potatoes

1) Boil the potatoes in salted water until they can be easily pierced with a fork. Drain thoroughly and place in a large bowl. By hand or with an electric mixer, mix in the butter; then add the milk, sour cream, and salt. Whip until the lumps are gone.

2) Remove the chili from oven and raise the oven temperature to 350°F. Use a spatula to carefully spread the potatoes over the chili, sealing the edges and making nice swirls. Sprinkle the cheese over the potatoes. Return the casserole to the oven and bake just until the cheese melts. Serve at once.

Cincinnati
Five-Way Chili

CINCINNATI IS A CITY BEWITCHED BY chili; there are at least a hundred joints in town that make a specialty of serving it. And we do mean *joints,* for chili, Cincinnati-style, tends to be one rude plate of food, best eaten off a Formica counter under humming fluorescent lights after midnight in the company of other devout chiliheads.

Bearing no resemblance to any southwestern-style bowl of red, this chili is called "five-way" because there are five separate layers in its full configuration. On a thick oval plate that has enough inward slope so the ingredients list toward the center, a base is created from a heap of glistening spaghetti noodles; they in turn are topped by a deliriously spiced sauce of finely ground beef, beans, raw onions, and finally a fluffy crown of Cheddar cheese. Oyster crackers are the traditional garnish, and the proper companion beverage is a milk shake or sweet soda pop.

No Cincinnati chili chef gives out his or her recipe, but we did manage to secure one by sending away a dollar to a lady just over the border in Kentucky, who advertised in the back of a midwestern housewife's magazine that she knew how to make the real thing. With some minor adjustments, it worked for us, and closely approximates some of the city's best brews. Feel free to fiddle and fuss to your own taste; and if you are missing cardamom or coriander, substitute something else. Five-way practically demands that you reinvent the recipe and make it your own.

NOTE: This recipe makes 4 servings.

1 $\frac{1}{4}$ pounds ground beef

2 medium onions, chopped

2 garlic cloves, minced

1 cup barbecue sauce

$\frac{1}{2}$ ounce unsweetened chocolate, grated

1 tablespoon chili powder

1 teaspoon freshly ground black pepper

$\frac{1}{4}$ teaspoon ground cumin

$\frac{1}{4}$ teaspoon ground turmeric

$\frac{1}{4}$ teaspoon ground allspice

$\frac{1}{4}$ teaspoon ground cinnamon

$\frac{1}{4}$ teaspoon ground cloves

$\frac{1}{4}$ teaspoon ground coriander

$\frac{1}{4}$ teaspoon ground cardamom

$\frac{1}{2}$ teaspoon salt

Tomato juice, as needed

9 ounces spaghetti

1 tablespoon butter

One 16-ounce can red kidney beans

1 pound Cheddar cheese, finely shredded

Oyster crackers, for garnish

1) In a large skillet or Dutch oven, brown the meat with half the chopped onions and the garlic, stirring to keep it loose. Drain any fat from the pan. Add the barbecue sauce and $\frac{1}{2}$ cup water and bring the mixture to a boil. Add the chocolate, spices, and salt. Cover and reduce the heat. Simmer 30 minutes, stirring occasionally. The chili will thicken as it cooks. Add tomato juice, as necessary, to create a brew that ladles up easily. Allow the chili to rest at least 30 minutes in a covered pan at room temperature. (Chili can be refrigerated and reheated to serve.)

2) Meanwhile, cook the spaghetti until just tender. Drain and toss with the butter. Rinse the beans and put into a small saucepan. Cook over medium heat until warm. Drain any excess liquid.

3) To make each plate, start with a layer of spaghetti; top it with the hot chili, and then a few warm beans and some of the remaining chopped onions. Pat on some cheese so the chili's heat can begin to melt it.

4) Serve immediately with oyster crackers.

16-Times World Champion Sirloin Chili

THE SINGLE TASTIEST MEAL WE EVER ate in Oklahoma was at the home of rodeo great and rancher Jim Shoulders, who holds the record for world championship gold buckles, with the sixteen he has earned for bronco and bull riding. Jim and his wife, Sharron, now raise a longhorn cattle cross called Salorn; and early one morning, while touting Salorn's leanness and health value, Sharron cooked up a memorable breakfast of breaded and skillet-fried Salorn steaks with cream gravy on the side. This was our idea of diet food!

At that moment, we knew that any chili representing the state of Oklahoma had to be one in which spice played second fiddle to high-quality beef, for beef is king in these parts: barbecued, air-dried for jerky, made into sausage or bologna, or carved into thick steaks and grilled over hardwood. This chili is firecracker hot; ideal for spooning atop slices of lusciously marbled beef.

If you are lucky enough to get Salorn beef for this recipe, it's perfect: low-fat, yet savory, and tender as a sigh. Another option is to order sirloins from The Cattlemen's restaurant in the stockyards of Fort Worth, (405) 236–0416. Or simply get the best cuts of sirloin or porterhouse you can find.

6 whole dried ancho chiles

4 whole dried chipotle chiles

4 garlic cloves, minced

2 tablespoons vegetable oil

$^1/_2$ cup tomato sauce

1 cup flat beer

2 teaspoons ground cumin

2 teaspoons salt

1 teaspoon dried Mexican oregano

1 tablespoon Worcestershire sauce

3 tablespoons packed brown sugar

1 tablespoon masa harina dissolved in $^1/_2$ cup water

2 to 3 pounds sirloin, porterhouse, and/or filet mignon

1) Place the chiles in a heatproof bowl and cover with boiling water. Let stand 30 minutes, until soft. Meanwhile, in a small skillet, sauté the garlic in the oil until golden. Seed and stem the chiles and place in a food processor or blender. Add the tomato sauce, beer, $^1/_2$ cup water, cumin, salt, oregano, Worcestershire sauce, brown sugar, and garlic. Puree thoroughly. Transfer the mixture to a saucepan. Stir in the masa harina mixture and bring to a simmer; cook 3 to 5 minutes.

2) Preheat the grill and grill the steak to taste. At the table, cut the steak into $^1/_2$-inch slices, and spoon chili puree over each serving of the meat.

3) This chili is great with beans and raw onion slices.

Let 'er Buck
Red Beer Chili

BETWEEN GO-ROUNDS AT THE PENDLE-
ton rodeo, we found something new to drink: red
beer. It sounds bizarre, but is in fact pretty damn good: a refreshing
blend of tap beer and canned tomato juice. Every bartender has a formula, which can range from a bubbly five-to-one, in which the tomato
juice barely flavors the beer, to a two-to-one blend reminiscent of a
juice-bar smoothie. During the rodeo, when the whole town goes cow-
boy-crazy, locals seem to enjoy red beer for breakfast, lunch, and supper. (*Brunch* is a seldom-heard term in these parts.)

Beef and beer and tomatoes are also the essence of many good
chili recipes, so we devised a formula that binds them together in a
spicy bowl of red that features the kind of seasonings that will inspire
you to holler the bronco rider's cry (and the Pendleton Round-Up
catch phrase), "Let 'er buck!"

2 dried chipotle chiles

4 dried ancho chiles

1 cup tomato sauce

One 12-ounce bottle of beer

1 cup chopped onions

2 garlic cloves, minced

2 tablespoons vegetable oil

2 pounds London broil, trimmed of fat and cut into $1/2$-inch cubes

$1 1/2$ teaspoons salt

1 teaspoon freshly ground black pepper

1 teaspoon ground cumin

1 tablespoon Worcestershire sauce

3 tablespoons prepared horseradish

Boiled potatoes

1) Place the chiles in a large heatproof bowl and cover with boiling water. Let stand 30 minutes, until soft; then seed and stem them. In a food processor or blender, puree the chiles with the tomato sauce and beer. Set aside.

2) In a large, heavy skillet or Dutch oven, sauté the onions and garlic in the oil until soft. Add the beef and cook until browned all over, stirring frequently. Add the chile puree and the remaining ingredients to the beef and simmer, uncovered, 20 minutes, stirring often.

3) This makes a soupy chili, best served in a bowl on a bed of smashed-up boiled potatoes.

Homage to Hershey Chocolate Chili

PENNSYLVANIA

THE SWEETEST SPOT IN THE WHOLE state of Pennsylvania is Hershey, where the air is perfumed with cocoa, and the main food group is chocolate. Hershey, of course, is where Hershey Bars and other chocolate candies are made; and although the town now sports shopping outlets, theme parks, and other tourist stuff, it is still basically a chocoholic's mecca; and it affords boundless opportunities to stuff yourself on Kisses and Krackle Bars and feel practically patriotic doing so.

Being chocolate lovers ourselves, we felt it obligatory to make Hershey, Pennsylvania, a part of this book. The idea of adding chocolate to chili is not weird at all. Mexican *mole* is built around it; and one of our favorite regional chilies, Cincinnati Five-Way Chili (page 111) is frequently spiked with chocolate.

Our homage to Hershey is a little bit chocolatey, but it packs enough pepper pow so that no one will mistake it for dessert!

1/3 cup chopped onions

2 garlic cloves, minced

2 tablespoons vegetable oil

2 pounds skinless, boneless chicken breasts, cut into 1-inch pieces (approximately 3 large whole breasts)

1 tablespoon salt

1/2 tablespoon freshly ground black pepper

1 teaspoon ground cumin

2 tablespoons unsweetened cocoa

One 14-ounce can chicken broth

One 15-ounce can tomato sauce

1/2 tablespoon red jalapeño powder

1 cup chopped fresh parsley

Two 15-ounce cans white kidney beans, drained

1 tablespoon masa harina dissolved in 1/4 cup water

2 tablespoons honey

1 cup sour cream

1) In a Dutch oven, sauté the onions and garlic in the oil until soft. Add the chicken and cook until browned. Remove from the heat. Add the salt, pepper, cumin, and cocoa, stirring well. Mix in the broth and 1 1/2 cups water, the tomato sauce, jalapeño powder, and parsley. Return to the heat and bring to a boil; cook at a very low boil, partially covered, for 35 minutes.

2) Add the beans and cook 15 minutes more. Add the masa harina mixture to the chili and cook 5 minutes more. Remove from the heat and stir in the honey and sour cream.

Chicken Chili and Cornmeal Parsley Dumplings

RHODE ISLAND

CHILI HAS EARNED A REPUTATION AS hot, spicy, assertive food. Such stereotypical recipe titles as Chain Gang Chili, Jailhouse Chili, Boar's Breath Chili, and Hellfire and Damnation Chili all suggest fare for the culinary daredevil with an asbestos palate and iron gut. But there are times when even the most macho among us needs a bowl of comfort food; and it is those times we suggest turning to this amiable chicken and dumpling chili inspired by two of Rhode Island's favorite things to eat: chicken and cornmeal, the latter in the form of tender little dumplings. This is a creamy, soothing chili with hardly any heat at all.

FOR THE CHILI

48 ounces canned chicken broth

3 pounds chicken parts, white and dark meat

3 tablespoons butter

2 bunches scallions, chopped (about 1 1/2 cups)

2 tablespoons all-purpose flour

1 cup warm milk

1 tablespoon chili powder

1 teaspoon salt

1 cup heavy cream

FOR THE CORNMEAL DUMPLINGS

1 cup white cornmeal

1/2 cup unbleached white flour

1 teaspoon baking powder

1/2 teaspoon salt

5 tablespoons cold butter, cut into pats

1/3 cup milk

1 egg, beaten

1/2 cup chopped fresh parsley

Make the chili

1) Place the chicken broth in a large skillet. Add the chicken parts and cook for 40 minutes, until tender. Drain the broth and reserve, keeping it warm. When the chicken is cool enough to handle, remove the skin and pick the meat from the bones. Discard the skin and bones, reserving the meat.

2) In a deep pot, melt the butter and sauté the scallions. Stir in the flour and mix well to form a paste. Gradually add 1 1/2 cups of the reserved chicken broth and the milk. Cook and stir until thickened. Stir in the chili powder and salt; add the heavy cream. Transfer the chili to a casserole and refrigerate while you prepare the dumplings. Refrigerate the remaining chicken broth.

Make the dumplings

1) In a food processor, mix together the cornmeal, flour, baking powder, and salt by pulsing for 10 seconds. Add the butter and pulse until crumbly. Add the milk, egg, and parsley and pulse just until the dough comes together. Don't overmix, or the dumplings will be tough. Place the dough in a lightly oiled bowl, cover, and refrigerate for at least 1 hour. (The dough can be chilled overnight.)

2) Reheat the chicken chili, covered in foil, in a low oven.

3) In a large saucepan, heat the reserved chicken broth, adding water, if necessary, to make about 6 cups of cooking liquid. Bring to a boil, then reduce the heat to a simmer. With well-floured hands, form 1-inch balls of the dumpling dough. Use a spoon to drop the balls of dumpling dough into the broth, one at a time. Partially cover the pot and simmer 5 to 7 minutes, until the dumplings rise to the surface.

4) To serve, ladle the chili into individual bowls and top with the dumplings. This dish should be served as soon as the dumplings are ready. This recipe makes about 10 dumplings.

Low-Country Chicken Chili

AUTHOR JOHN MARTIN TAYLOR—AKA Hoppin' John—has been a guiding light for the culinary reawakening of Charleston, South Carolina, over the last several years. Author of the exhilarating *Hoppin' John's Lowcountry Cooking; The New Southern Cook;* and most recently, *Fearless Frying,* Mr. Taylor is also proprietor of Hoppin' John's bookstore, which carries not only books about food and cooking but also utterly delicious, locally made cornmeal, corn flour, chowchow, and green tomato relish. We have become addicted to the grits he sells, which are ground to his specifications and which make the most delicious "creamy grits" on earth.

We love to cook and serve a high-flavored chicken chili similar to the one in Hoppin' John's book, with creamy grits on the side to sop up the opaque gravy. He notes that Tex-Mex flavors have been part of Deep South cookery since long before they were trendy; and the use of peppers has long been a tradition in low-country cooking.

FOR THE CREAMY
GRITS

4 cups water or chicken
broth

4 tablespoons butter

1 cup stone-ground grits

2 to 3 cups milk or half-
and-half

FOR THE CHILI

2 dried ancho chiles

1 1/2 cups dried pinto or
kidney beans, soaked
overnight and drained

8 cups chicken broth

3 large carrots, peeled

2 large onions, cut in half

1 bay leaf

1/2 teaspoon crushed
dried thyme

One 28-ounce can
crushed tomatoes

2 large chicken breasts
on the bone

Salt, freshly ground black
pepper, and Tabasco to
taste

Make the grits

If you are going to serve this chili with grits, start
cooking the grits first. Place the water and butter
in a heavy-bottom stockpot. Bring to a boil and
stir in the grits. Return to the boil and reduce the
heat to a simmer for 12 to 15 minutes, stirring
often, until the grits thicken. Stir in about 1/2 cup
of the milk and simmer the grits another 10 minutes, stirring often. Keep adding milk, 1/2 cup at a
time, every 10 minutes and keep stirring the grits.
They will continue to thicken and absorb the
milk. Cook for a minimum total of 1 hour,
preferably 2 hours, at the lowest possible simmer,
stirring frequently. When served, the grits should
be thick enough so they don't run, but moist
enough to require a spoon rather than a fork.

Make the chili

1) Place the chiles in a large heatproof bowl and cover with boiling water. Let stand 30 minutes, until soft; then seed and stem them. Set aside.

2) Place the beans, broth, carrots, onions, bay leaf, and thyme in a large stockpot and bring to a simmer. Simmer 40 minutes, stirring occasionally.

3) Remove the carrots and onions from the broth and set them aside to cool. Remove $\frac{1}{2}$ cup of the beans and place them in a food processor. Add the chiles, two of the cooked onion halves, and 1 cup of the crushed tomatoes. Puree.

4) Add the puree and the remaining tomatoes to the stockpot and bring to a simmer. Add the chicken breasts. Cook 1 hour, or until tender. Remove the chicken from the pot, and when it is cool enough to handle, remove and discard the skin and bones. Pull the meat into large shreds and return the shreds to the stockpot. Dice the reserved carrots and onion halves. Add them to the pot. Season to taste with salt, pepper, and Tabasco. Simmer 5 to 10 minutes.

5) This is a fairly soupy chili. Serve in a bowl with the hot creamy grits or rice.

Roughneck Boilermaker Chili

SOUTH DAKOTA

THE ANNUAL CONVENTION OF BIKERS IN Sturgis, South Dakota, attracts all manner of man and woman with a passion for two-wheeling on the open road. Among them is an acquaintance whom we'll call Biker Bob to protect his anonymity. You see, Biker Bob is a mild-mannered corporate executive five days a week; but on Saturday and Sunday, he takes his leather and denim out of the closet, threads a ring in one earlobe, fires up his hog, and rides wild and free with a gang of fellow Harley aficionados.

Biker Bob occasionally invites us to dinner at his nice suburban home, where his déclassé biker attitude combines with surprisingly fussy middle-class culinary skills to create this in-your-face chili. Beer, bourbon, beans, onions, garlic: It's a veritable checklist of outlaw ingredients! Bob claims he learned the recipe from another biker one year at the Sturgis rally. Wherever it came from, it's become a staple around our house for those occasions when we want chili with major attitude.

$^1/_2$ cup chopped onion

2 garlic cloves, minced

1 $^1/_2$ tablespoons vegetable oil

1 $^1/_2$ pounds ground round

One 15 $^1/_2$-ounce can pinto beans, drained and rinsed

One 14 $^1/_2$-ounce can diced tomatoes

1 teaspoon salt

2 teaspoons dried Mexican oregano

1 $^1/_4$ cups beer

1 shot of Jack Daniel's whiskey

2 tablespoons chili powder (we use Pendery's Dallas Dynamite, see p. 9)

1 teaspoon freshly ground black pepper

2 teaspoons sugar

1 tablespoon masa harina dissolved in $^1/_4$ cup warm water

Tortilla chips

1 red onion, chopped

1 cup grated sharp Cheddar cheese

1) In a large skillet or Dutch oven, sauté the onion and garlic in the oil until soft. Add the meat and cook until browned, stirring to keep it broken up. Drain any excess fat from pan.

2) Add the beans, tomatoes, salt, oregano, beer, whiskey, chili powder, pepper, and sugar. Bring to simmer and cook, uncovered, for 30 minutes, stirring frequently. Stir in the masa harina mixture and cook 7 to 10 minutes more.

3) Serve on a bed of tortilla chips, sprinkled with the onion and cheese.

Memphis Barbecue Shrimp Chili

MEMPHIS HAS A WELL-DESERVED reputation as America's Porkopolis for all the fine ribs and chopped-meat sandwiches to be found in its barbecue restaurants. But a lesser-appreciated culinary gift of the City on the Bluff is wickedly delicious shrimp or, as the locals pronounce it, *swimp*. In particular, we are thinking of a dish called barbecued shrimp, as served at Gridley's on Summer Avenue—a messy, peel-'em-yourself affair in which the shrimp are cosseted in a tongue-tickling hot barbecue sauce. Years ago, we learned to make a good, chili-spiked facsimile of that sauce for any time we get a stash of good shrimp at home. This is a little less sloppy than the Memphis version, as we like to peel the shrimp before cooking. That way, once the dish is served, there's no fussing; the only thing you need to concentrate on is eating.

1 1/2 pounds medium shrimp

4 tablespoons unsalted butter

3 tablespoons olive oil

5 garlic cloves, coarsely chopped

1 1/2 cups barbecue sauce

1 tablespoon Worcestershire sauce

1 teaspoon hot sauce (Tabasco or similar brand)

1 teaspoon liquid smoke

1 1/2 teaspoons crushed red pepper flakes

1 1/2 teaspoons salt

1 teaspoon freshly ground coarse black pepper

1 tablespoon chili powder

1/2 cup chopped fresh parsley

1 lemon, sliced very thin

White rice and/or French bread

1) Peel and clean the shrimp. Melt the butter and oil in a large, heavy skillet. Add the garlic and sauté until soft. Add the shrimp and cook until pink. Add the barbecue, Worcestershire, and hot sauces, the liquid smoke, red pepper flakes, salt, black pepper, and chili powder. Simmer 10 minutes. Add the parsley and lemon slices. Simmer 5 to 7 minutes longer.

2) This makes a soupy, saucy chili. Serve on white rice to absorb the gravy or with chunks of French bread for dipping.

Tigua Indian Definitive Bowl of Red

IN THE MID-1970S WE WERE CRUISING through El Paso and stopped to look around the urban reservation of the Tigua (say *Tee-wa)* Indians. These indigenous people make beautiful pottery and even more beautiful chili.

While we were strolling around the cafeteria, we met Jose Sierra, the tribe's chief. Pegging us as out-of-towners, Mr. Sierra kindly suggested that we'd be wise *not* to order the chili. He thought it would be too hot for our gentle palates. His warning was a cry to arms, so of course, we ordered two big bowls. As we ate them with tears streaming from our eyes and beads of sweat popping out on our foreheads, we came to know two things: one, the Tiguas make the best chili in west Texas; and two, it is not wise to play macho games with Texas Indian chiliheads. You will lose.

After the heat on our tongues subsided enough for us to regain the power of speech, we begged Mr. Sierra to get us the recipe. Here it is, but toned down to mid-level hot. If you want to goose it up to tear-wrenching Tigua standards, double the jalapeño pepper powder.

1 cup chopped onions

2 garlic cloves, minced

2 tablespoons vegetable oil

2 pounds beef round, cut into $1/2$-inch cubes

$1^1/_2$ teaspoons salt

1 tablespoon sugar

$1^1/_2$ teaspoons freshly ground black pepper

$1^1/_2$ teaspoons ground dried Mexican oregano

1 tablespoon ground cumin

5 tablespoons chili powder

$1^1/_2$ teaspoons red jalapeño powder

One 15-ounce can tomato sauce

1 tablespoon masa harina dissolved in $1/2$ cup water

Cooked beans, rice, or bread

Sour cream

1) In a large skillet or Dutch oven, sauté the onions and garlic in the oil until soft. Add the beef and cook until browned. Add the salt, sugar, pepper, oregano, cumin, chili powder, jalapeño powder, tomato sauce, and 1 ½ cups water; stir well. Bring to a boil. Reduce the heat to a low simmering boil and cook, partially covered, for 1 hour 10 minutes. Remove from the heat. Add the masa harina mixture. Return to low heat and cook, stirring occasionally, 5 minutes.

2) Serve with beans, rice, or bread on the side: all useful for muffling the heat. Also helpful is a tablespoon of sour cream.

Navajo Lamb and Golden Hominy Chili

TO THE NAVAJO COOK, CORN IS NOT ONLY a sacrament but the basis of a good meal. And because many Navajos are sheepherders, lamb or mutton is at least as popular as beef. Travel through Navajo country, from Window Rock, Arizona, to the rapturous landscape of Monument Valley at the Utah border, and you can sample a wide array of indigenous Native American stews and other dishes made with corn and lamb.

To the jaded chilihead palate, many of these Native American foods can seem bland. We have often eaten a simple bowl of mutton and hominy stew in a roadside cafe, marveling at its earthy character . . . but secretly wishing we had a pocketful of fiery chiles to add to it and give it zest. And so, inspired by some of the best Native American dishes we have tasted on and off the reservations, we created this chili based on the fundamental ingredients of lamb and corn but with the addition of a little heat to please those whose tongues yearn for the chile pepper's kick.

1 dried pasilla chile

2 large dried ancho chiles

3 dried habanero chiles

$^1/_4$ cup chopped onion

4 garlic cloves, minced

2 tablespoons corn oil

2 pounds lamb, trimmed of fat and gristle and cut into $^1/_2$-inch cubes

$^1/_2$ tablespoon salt

$1^1/_2$ teaspoons ground cumin

1 tablespoon sugar

One 15$^1/_2$-ounce can diced tomatoes with roasted garlic

One 10-ounce package frozen corn kernels

One 15$^1/_2$-ounce can golden hominy, drained

1 tablespoon masa harina dissolved in $^1/_4$ cup water

1) Place the chiles in a large heatproof bowl and cover with boiling water. Let stand 30 minutes, until soft; then seed and stem them. In a food processor or blender, puree the chiles with 1 cup water. Set aside.

2) In a Dutch oven, sauté the onion and garlic in the oil. Cook until soft. Add the lamb and cook until browned. Add the chili puree, salt, cumin, sugar, tomatoes, and a tomato can full of water. Bring to a boil and reduce the heat to a low simmer. Cook, partially covered, 45 minutes, stirring occasionally. Remove from the heat and stir in the corn and hominy. Cook, uncovered, over low heat for 15 minutes more. Add the masa harina mixture and cook 5 minutes more.

Maple-Spiked Chili with Cheddar Stars

Winter in Vermont inevitably conjures images of warm woolen shirts, crackling fireplaces, steaming cups of mulled cider, and satisfying bowls of hot chili.

Good Vermont foodstuffs include plenty of indigenous beans and hoops of store cheese, both of which are fundamental ingredients for a wonderful, warming kind of chili that bears little resemblance to a southwestern bowl of red, but is true in heart and soul to the spirit of Green Mountain life. Most chilies made with beans benefit from a little sweetening to balance the intrinsic heat of the pod. What better way to get that sweetness than a liberal infusion of pure Vermont maple syrup?

Please use 100% pure maple syrup in this recipe, *not* imitation maple syrup.

1 pound dried cranberry beans

1 cup chopped onions

2 garlic cloves, minced

2 tablespoons vegetable oil

2 pounds ground chuck

1 tablespoon maple pepper (from Green Market, p. 8)

1 1/2 teaspoons salt

3 tablespoons chili powder

1 teaspoon ground allspice

One 15-ounce can tomato sauce

1/2 cup pure maple syrup

Twelve 2 × 2 × 1/4-inch slices sharp Cheddar cheese

1) Soak the beans overnight; pick out and discard any bad beans and stones. Rinse the beans and place in a large pot with fresh water. Cook about 1 hour, until tender. Drain and reserve 4 cups of the beans. If you have extra, you can serve them on the side or use in other recipes.

2) In a Dutch oven, sauté the onion and garlic in the oil until soft. Add the meat, stirring to keep it loose and crumbly, and cook until browned through. Add the maple pepper, salt, chili powder, allspice, tomato sauce, maple syrup, and 2 cups water. Bring to a boil; reduce

the heat to a very low simmer and cook, partially covered, for 30 minutes. Add the reserved beans, and cook 15 minutes more.

3) Use a 1½-inch-wide star-shaped cookie cutter to cut stars from the cheese slices or cut the stars freehand with a small sharp knife. To serve, spoon the chili into bowls and top each with 2 or 3 stars and a sprinkle of maple pepper.

Shenandoah Valley Apple-Nut Chili

BEYOND GREAT HAM, BARBECUE, CRAB-cakes, spoonbread, and Brunswick stew, Virginia has many other culinary treasures. Whenever we travel through the Shenandoah Valley, we make it our business to eat as many locally grown peanuts and apples as possible, for both are delicious native crops.

After one recent trip, with a trunk full of autumn's apples and a few quarts of good Virginia peanuts, we decided to combine the two with the Old Dominion's proclivity for good pork. The result was one luscious bowl of chili, built on a puree of hot pasilla pods.

2 pound pork loin

6 dried pasilla chiles

2 Granny Smith apples

1 cup chicken broth

2 tablespoons creamy peanut butter

1 cup chopped onions

2 tablespoons peanut oil

2 teaspoons ground ginger

2 teaspoons dry mustard

1 teaspoon salt

1 tablespoon packed brown sugar

$^1/_2$ cup apple cider

1 bunch scallions, chopped (about $^2/_3$ cup)

Cooked rice

1) Preheat the oven to 350°F. Place the pork in an uncovered baking pan and roast for at least 1 hour, until cooked through. Don't turn it and don't season it as it cooks. When cool enough to handle, cut the meat into bite-sized pieces.

2) Place the chiles in a large heatproof bowl and cover with boiling water. Let stand 30 minutes, until soft; then seed and stem them. Place the chiles in a food processor. Peel, core, and quarter one of the apples and add it to the chiles along with $^1/_2$ cup of the broth and the peanut butter. Puree until smooth; set aside.

3) In a Dutch oven, sauté the onions in the oil until soft. Add the chile puree, ginger, mustard, salt, brown sugar, and cider. Stir and bring to a simmer. Add the pork along with the remaining $1/2$ cup chicken broth, if needed to keep the mixture good and moist. Cook and stir until the pork is warmed through.

4) Dice the remaining apple and mix it with the scallions. Use this garnish to top each serving of chili. Serve with rice on the side.

Seattle Coffee Chili

EVEN BEFORE THE STARBUCKS JUG-gernaut, Seattle had a solid reputation as the coffee capital of the United States, with hundreds of independent coffee shops and little *latte* wagons on every street corner.

There are few nicer marriages than that of coffee to chili. Chuck-wagon cooks have known this fact for years, spiking their *con carnes* with a splash or two from the morning coffeepot. We thought about this good idea and figured it would make sense to substitute skinless chicken for beef (out of respect for Seattle's powerful streak of nutritional correctness), and to accent the coffee flavor by using dark, smoky pasilla peppers. The result is a simple but sophisticated chili that is low in fat and high in flavor.

12 large dried pasilla chiles

1 1/4 cups very strong black coffee brewed from a dark roast (French roast works for us)

One 13 3/4-ounce can chicken broth

1/2 cup chopped onion

1 garlic clove, smashed

2 tablespoons vegetable oil

2 pounds skinless, boneless chicken, cut in 1/2-inch cubes

1 tablespoon chili powder

1 tablespoon sugar

1 tablespoon salt

1 tablespoon masa harina dissolved in 1/4 cup warm water

1) Place the chiles in a large heatproof bowl and cover with boiling water. Let stand for 30 minutes, until soft; then stem and seed them. In a food processor or blender, puree the chiles with the coffee and chicken broth until smooth. Set aside.

2) In a Dutch oven, sauté the onion and garlic in the oil until soft. Add the chicken and stir and cook until browned. Add the chile puree. Stir in the chili powder, sugar, and salt. Bring to a boil, reduce the heat, and simmer, partially covered, for 1 hour. Remove from the heat and stir in the masa harina mixture. Return to the heat and cook for an additional 7 minutes.

Fried Bologna Chili

FRIED BOLOGNA IS THE HOUSE SPECIALTY of cafés throughout West Virginia: thin slices sizzled on the griddle to go with morning eggs; thicker ones for sandwiches with coleslaw at lunch; and thick chunks, skillet browned, to go with beans and corn bread for a hearty supper.

We'll admit that bologna appreciation is a fairly advanced talent, even for devoted connoisseurs of what a French critic might refer to as America's *cuisine maudite*. But most gastronomes who turn up their noses know it only as lunch meat, served cold in thin slices on Wonder bread with Miracle Whip. Not to impugn such a fine and, in its own way, perfect sandwich, we humbly submit that when it is fried to a crisp, bologna develops a whole new, wickedly tasty character. So even if you are a bologna frowner, try this chili ode to West Virginia and see if you don't come to count the springy-bodied pink stuff as your newfound friend.

3 garlic cloves, minced

1/2 cup diced onion

2 tablespoons vegetable oil

1 pound thick-cut bologna (from the deli counter at the market), diced into 1/4-inch cubes

One 28-ounce can crushed tomatoes

1 cup barbecue sauce

2 tablespoons chili powder

1 teaspoon ground cumin

1 teaspoon freshly ground black pepper

1 ounce unsweetened chocolate, cut or broken into small pieces

Two 15 1/2-ounce cans red kidney beans, drained and rinsed

White bread

1) In a heavy skillet or Dutch oven, sauté the garlic and onion in the oil until soft. Add the bologna. Cook and stir until the meat is browned. Add 2 cups of the tomatoes, the barbecue sauce, chili powder, cumin, pepper, and chocolate. Mix together and cook 10 minutes, adding more of the tomatoes, if needed to keep the chili loose. Add the beans and cook until they are well heated.

2) Serve in a bowl with a stack of soft white bread on the side for mopping and sopping.

Green Bay Chili

CHILI JOHN'S HAS BEEN A LANDMARK in Green Bay, Wisconsin, since 1913, when a Lithuanian immigrant named John Isaac opened a diner featuring his favorite one-dish meal. By mid-century, Chili John's unique blend of spicy oil and meat sauce, as well as his layered configuration with beans and noodles, had become a favorite dish throughout Wisconsin.

Green Bay–style chili is architectonically similar to Cincinnati Five-Way Chili, but the addition of spicy hot oil gives it a special sparkle. The original recipe is still a secret formula guarded by Chili John's descendants; but if you need to savor the original stuff and can't get to the restaurant in Green Bay, the chili can be shipped anywhere—just call them (414) 336–8043. Otherwise, this recipe replicates Green Bay chili in spirit, if not in precise proportions.

As a historical note, Chili John's family boasts that John has another claim to fame. He was the man responsible for the creation of tiny, spoon-sized oyster crackers. He felt the old-fashioned store cracker, at least 1 inch in diameter, was too unwieldy to garnish his chili, so he convinced the cracker manufacturers to downsize.

FOR THE CHILI

$^1/_2$ cup chopped onion

2 tablespoons vegetable oil

2 pounds ground chuck

1 $^1/_2$ teaspoons salt

$^1/_2$ teaspoon freshly ground black pepper

1 teaspoon Worcestershire sauce

5 to 10 drops Tabasco, to taste

1 $^1/_3$ cups barbecue sauce

FOR THE SPICY OIL

$^1/_2$ cup olive oil

1 tablespoon chili powder

$^1/_2$ teaspoon ground cumin

$^1/_2$ teaspoon ground coriander

$^1/_4$ teaspoon ground cardamom

2 garlic cloves, finely minced

Make the chili

In a large skillet, sauté the onion in the oil until soft. Add the beef; cook and stir until browned, separating the meat so it remains crumbly rather than cloddish. Drain off all excess fat. Season with the salt, pepper, Worcestershire sauce, and Tabasco. Stir in the barbecue sauce and simmer over medium-low heat 5 minutes, stirring to mix.

Make the spicy oil

Combine the oil with the chili powder, cumin, coriander, and cardamom. Heat this mixture to a simmer in a small skillet. Stir in the garlic and cook until soft. Stir half of the spicy oil into the

FOR THE CHILI'S BED

12 ounces spaghetti noodles

1 tablespoon butter

One 16-ounce can kidney beans

1 large onion, chopped

TOPPINGS

Shredded Cheddar cheese

Sour cream

Oyster crackers

chili; reserve the remaining oil. Keep the meat mixture warm.

Assemble the chili

1) Cook the spaghetti until just tender. Drain and toss with the butter and keep warm. Rinse the beans and place in a small saucepan. Add $\frac{1}{2}$ cup water and cook over medium heat until warm; drain well.

2) To serve, arrange the noodles on 4 to 6 plates. Top each serving with beans and chopped onion. Ladle the chili over all and add the reserved spicy oil to taste. Sprinkle toppings over, as desired.

Code 10 Chili

LIVED WITH A WOMAN NAMED MARCIA Novato in New Mexico," explained Steve Rankin, proprietor of The Noon Break, a comfy little café off the main street of Cody, Wyoming. "Marcia was a Navajo, and it was with her I discovered the joy of chili. But I moved on and came to Wyoming. When I arrived, I realized there was no real chili to eat, at least nothing like I had grown to love in New Mexico. So I remembered how we made it and put it on my menu. Marcia and I always made it with chicken, but you can use any kind of meat you like, or no meat at all."

We like it best with sausage, as indicated below. It is a fairly soupy chili, best eaten with a spoon and a stack of tortillas on the side for dipping and mopping.

2 cups chopped onions

$^1/_3$ cup peanut oil

4 garlic cloves, minced

$^1/_4$ cup all-purpose flour

One 14$^1/_2$-ounce can chicken broth

Four 4$^1/_2$-ounce cans chopped green chiles, with liquid

2 cups diced red-skinned potato, skin on

1 to 2 jalapeño or habanero peppers, seeded and diced, optional

2 tablespoons chili powder

$^1/_2$ teaspoon salt

$^1/_2$ teaspoon freshly ground black pepper

$^1/_2$ teaspoon dried Mexican oregano

1 pound sweet pork sausage, cooked and crumbled

Flour tortillas

1) In a heavy skillet, sauté the onions in the oil until soft. Add the garlic, then sprinkle in the flour, stirring constantly. Cook and stir over medium heat 3 to 5 minutes, until the onions just barely begin to brown.

2) Stir in the broth, green chiles, potatoes, jalapeño peppers (if using), chili powder, salt, black pepper, and oregano. Simmer 20 to 30 minutes, stirring and scraping the bottom of the skillet so the mixture doesn't stick, until the potatoes are soft. Add the sausage and cook 5 minutes more.

3) Serve with soft flour tortillas on the side.

Side Dishes

Although many of the chilies in this book are one-dish meals, requiring nothing more than something to drink on the side, some of the simpler recipes do allow the companionship of other foods. Generally, plain white rice or simple beans are ideal on the side if the chili itself is beanless. Green salad or coleslaw is good to accompany chilies that are mostly meat. And warm flour tortillas or squares of corn bread are almost always welcome for sopping up good gravy. The following are a few basic side-dish recipes suitable to accompany chili.

Perfect Simple Guacamole

3 large ripe avocados

Juice of 1 lemon

Juice of 1 lime

1 teaspoon salt

2 garlic cloves, finely minced

Tortilla chips

While we have nothing against zesty, chock-full kinds of guacamole, it is our belief that when guacamole is served as an hors d'oeuvre before something as complex as chili, it should be simple, clear, and not too hot: a culinary analogy to the sort of stretching exercises athletes do before the main event. This recipe fills that bill.

1) In a medium bowl, mash the avocados with the lemon and lime juices, salt, and garlic using a potato masher or large spoon. Do not overmash, just enough to combine the ingredients. A hunk or two of unblended avocado is just fine.

2) Serve with crisp tortilla chips.

Three-Bean Salad

1/3 cup red wine vinegar

1/2 cup olive oil

2 tablespoons freshly squeezed lemon juice

2 garlic cloves, minced

2 teaspoons salt

1 teaspoon ground cumin

2 teaspoons chili powder

1/4 cup diced red onion

1 tablespoon sugar

1 jalapeño pepper, seeded and minced, optional

One 15 1/2-ounce can kidney beans, drained and rinsed

One 15 1/2-ounce can chickpeas, drained and rinsed

2 cups fresh green beans, cut into 1-inch pieces, blanched and cooled

1/2 cup finely diced carrot

2/3 cup finely diced green bell pepper

2/3 cup finely diced red bell pepper

Even those Rio Grande purists who say that chili must be a strictly beef dish, without beans, allow that beans *served on the side* make a good companion for the taste of the chile pepper.

Complex chilies are best accompanied by the most basic beans, which provide a clear, starchy balance to the fire and spice: kidney beans, pinto beans, white beans, pink beans, and black beans. Less elaborate recipes can benefit from an accompanying bean salad that has its own spices that echo the flavor of the chili. A good example is this fiesta-colorful three-bean salad, long a favorite around our house for barbecue as well as chili. Note that it is best to make it at least a few hours in advance and let the beans marinate in the vinaigrette before serving.

1) In a small bowl, combine the vinegar, oil, lemon juice, garlic, salt, cumin, chili powder, onion, sugar, and, if desired, jalapeño pepper. Whisk together well.

2) In a large bowl, combine the kidney beans, chickpeas, green beans, carrot, and bell peppers. Pour the dressing over the bean mixture and stir thoroughly but gently. Cover and allow to season 2 hours at room temperature before serving. The salad may be refrigerated a day or two, but bring it to room temperature before serving.

Corn Pudding

4 eggs, beaten

1 stick butter, melted

1 cup heavy cream

1 teaspoon salt

$^1/_3$ cup sugar

$^1/_2$ cup all-purpose flour

Pinch cayenne

Two 14$^1/_2$-ounce cans creamed corn (do not use unsalted corn)

Two 10-ounce boxes frozen corn niblets, semithawed

This is one of the great recipes of all time. We learned it years ago from a dear old friend, Ippy Patterson, who learned it years before that from a friend of hers in San Francisco. It is rich, creamy, and impossible to stop eating. Although not appropriate as a side dish for thick chilies with lots of vegetables, it is wonderful alongside more spartan ones of pork or beef.

Preheat the oven to 350°F. In a large bowl, mix together all of the ingredients, except the creamed corn and corn niblets. Gently mix in the creamed corn. Mix in the corn niblets last, taking care not to crush the kernels. Pour into an un-greased heatproof baking dish, about 13 × 9 × 2 inches. Bake 1 hour, until the top is golden and the custard is set.

Jalapeño Corn Bread

3 eggs, beaten

$^1/_4$ cup corn oil

1 tablespoon baking powder

1 cup grated sharp Cheddar cheese

2 cups yellow cornmeal (preferably stone ground)

1 cup all-purpose flour

One 14$^1/_2$-ounce can creamed corn (do not use unsalted corn)

1 cup whole milk

1$^1/_2$ tablespoons sugar

$^1/_2$ tablespoon salt

$^1/_2$ cup sour cream

One 4$^1/_2$-ounce can chopped and seeded jalapeño peppers

1) Preheat the oven to 350°F. Grease a 14 × 11-inch baking pan.

2) Place all the ingredients in a large mixing bowl and blend. Do not overmix, or the corn bread will be leathery. Pour the batter into the prepared pan and bake for 40 minutes, until the top is golden brown and a knife inserted into the center comes out clean.

Coleslaw

$^1/_2$ cup mayonnaise

$^1/_4$ cup white vinegar

2 tablespoons sour cream or plain yogurt

1 tablespoon celery seed

1 teaspoon salt

$^1/_4$ cup sugar

$^1/_4$ to $^1/_2$ cup milk, as needed

1 cup shredded carrot

4 cups finely shredded green cabbage

In a large mixing bowl, combine all the ingredients, except the milk, carrots, and cabbage. Stir to blend; add just enough milk so the mixture is the consistency of house paint. Stir in the carrots and cabbage. Add more salt, if desired.

Index

A

Ale. *See* Beer/Ale
Almonds
    Havana Moon Chili, 42–43
American Chop Suey Chili, 68–70
Anaheim chiles, 11. *See also*
    California chiles; Chiles
Ancho chiles, 12. *See also* Chiles
    Bluegrass Burgoo Chili, 62–64
    Buffalo Beef and Weck Chili, 104–5
    Georgia Pork and Peanut Chili, 44–45
    Highway 61 Chili, 82–83
    Let 'er Buck Red Beef Chili, 118–19
    Line Camp Chili and Biscuits, 21–23
    Low-Country Chicken Chili, 125–27
    Mule-Kicking Hot Chili, 84–85
    Navaho Lamb and Golden Hominy
        Chili, 134–35
    Paniolo Macadamia Nut and Chipotle
        Chili, 46–47
    Pig Chili, 106–7
    16-Times World Champion Sirloin
        Chili, 115–17
    Venison Chili with Snowcap Beans,
        33–35
    Yankee Bean Pot Chili, 95–97
Apple-Nut Chili, Shenandoah Valley,
    139–41
Avocados
    Perfect Simple Guacamole, 154

B

Barbecue sauce
    Bluegrass Burgoo Chili, 62–64
    Church Supper Chili Mac and Cheese,
        89–92
    Cincinnati Five-Way Chili, 111–14

    Fried Bologna Chili, 144–45
    Green Bay Chili, 146–49
    Highway 61 Chili, 82–83
    Hot Springs Chili-Tamale Spread,
        26–29
    Memphis Barbecue Shrimp Chili,
        130–31
    Roadhouse Barbecue Sauce, 6–7
    Yankee Bean Pot Chili, 95–97
Basil
    Gilroy Super Garlic Chili, 30–32
    Herb Garden Springtime Chili, 36–37
Beans, canned or dried
    Café Brenda Black Bean Vegetable
        Chili, 78–81
    Chicagoland Chili Mac, 51–52
    Chili à Whistle Stop, 18–20
    Chili of the Garden State, 98–99
    cooking, 5
    Cowboy Poetry Chili, 93–94
    Fried Bologna Chili, 144–45
    Green Bay Chili, 146–49
    Havana Moon Chili, 42–43
    Homage to Hershey Chocolate Chili,
        120–21
    Hot Springs Chili-Tamale Spread,
        26–29
    Low-Country Chicken Chili, 125–27
    Maple-Spiked Chili with Cheddar
        Stars, 136–38
    Mardi Gras Vegetable Chili, 65–67
    Porubsky's Grocery Store Chili,
        58–61
    Rock-Ribbed Bean-and-Beef Chili,
        73–74
    Roughneck Boilermaker Chili, 128–29
    soaking and cooking, 5
    Three-Bean Salad, 155

Venison Chili with Snowcap Beans,
33–35
Yankee Bean Pot Chili, 95–97
Beans, green
Three-Bean Salad, 155
Beans, lima
Bluegrass Burgoo Chili, 62–64
Blue Hen Succotash Chili, 38–39
Beef
Buffalo Beef and Weck Chili, 104–5
Gilroy Super Garlic Chili, 30–32
ground
American Chop Suey Chili,
68–70
Chicagoland Chili Mac, 51–52
Chili à Whistle Stop, 18–20
Church Supper Chili Mac and
Cheese, 89–92
Cincinnati Five-Way Chili,
111–14
Forty Below Meat Loaf and
Mashed Potatoes Chili, 108–10
Green Bay Chili, 146–49
Havana Moon Chili, 42–43
Hot Springs Chili-Tamale
Spread, 26–29
Maple-Spiked Chili with
Cheddar Stars, 136–38
Porubsky's Grocery Store Chili,
58–61
Rock-Ribbed Bean-and-Beef
Chili, 73–74
Roughneck Boilermaker Chili,
128–29
Let 'er Buck Red Beef Chili,
118–19
Mesilla Valley Bowl of Green,
100–3
Mule-Kicking Hot Chili, 84–85
Serious Capitol Punishment
Chili, 40–41
sirloin

16-Times World Champion
Sirloin Chili, 115–17
Chili Coeur d'Alene, 48–50
Cornish Miner Chili Pasties,
75–77
Line Camp Chili and Biscuits,
21–23
Tigua Indian Definitive Bowl of
Red, 132–33
Beer/Ale
Let 'er Buck Red Beef Chili, 118–19
Line Camp Chili and Biscuits, 21–23
Mule-Kicking Hot Chili, 84–85
Roughneck Boilermaker Chili, 128–29
Serious Capitol Punishment Chili,
40–41
16-Times World Champion Sirloin
Chili, 115–17
Bell peppers
Chili of the Garden State, 98–99
roasting, 5–6
Three-Bean Salad, 155
Biscuits, Line Camp Chili and, 21–23
Black beans. *See also* Beans, canned or dried
Café Brenda Vegetable Black Bean
Chili, 78–81
Havana Moon Chili, 42–43
Bluegrass Burgoo Chili, 62–64
Blue Hen Succotash Chili, 38–39
Bologna Chili, Fried, 144–45
Buffalo Beef and Weck Chili, 104–5

C

Cabbage
Coleslaw, 158
Café Brenda Black Bean Vegetable Chili,
78–81
California chiles. *See also* Anaheim chiles;
Chiles
Chili Coeur d'Alene, 48–50

Gilroy Super Garlic Chili, 30–32

Mardi Gras Vegetable Chili, 65–67

Carrots

Blue Hen Succotash Chili, 38–39

Coleslaw, 158

Cornish Miner Chili Pasties, 75–77

Line Camp Chili and Biscuits, 21–23

Low-Country Chicken Chili, 125–27

Sunday Supper Chicken Chili, 53–55

Three-Bean Salad, 155

Cheddar cheese

American Chop Suey Chili, 68–70

Church Supper Chili Mac and Cheese, 89–92

Cincinnati Five-Way Chili, 111–14

Forty Below Meat Loaf and Mashed Potatoes Chili, 108–10

Jalapeño Corn Bread, 157

Maple-Spiked Chili with Cheddar Stars, 136–38

Rock-Ribbed Bean-and-Beef Chili, 73–74

Roughneck Boilermaker Chili, 128–29

Cheese. *See* Cheddar cheese

Chesapeake Bay Chili, 71–72

Chicagoland Chili Mac, 51–52

Chicken

Bluegrass Burgoo Chili, 62–64

Blue Hen Succotash Chili, 38–39

Chicken Chili and Cornmeal Parsley Dumplings, 122–24

Herb Garden Springtime Chili, 36–37

Homage to Hershey Chocolate Chili, 120–21

Low-Country Chicken Chili, 125–27

Seattle Coffee Chili, 142–43

Sunday Supper Chicken Chili, 53–55

Chickpeas. *See also* Beans, canned or dried

Three-Bean Salad, 155

Chiles. *See also* Green chiles; *specific kinds*

handling, 4–6

rehydrating dried, 4–5

roasting, 5–6

types of, 11–13

Chili cook-offs, 14–15

Chili Coeur d'Alene, 48–50

Chili of the Garden State, 98–99

Chili à la Whistle Stop, 18–20

Chipotle chiles, 12. *See also* Chiles

Bluegrass Burgoo Chili, 62–64

Highway 61 Chili, 82–83

Let 'er Buck Red Beef Chili, 118–19

Line Camp Chili and Biscuits, 21–23

Mule-Kicking Hot Chili, 84–85

Paniolo Macadamia Nut and Chipotle Chili, 46–47

Pig Chili, 106–7

16-Times World Champion Sirloin Chili, 115–17

Chocolate/cocoa

Café Brenda Black Bean Vegetable Chili, 78–81

Cincinnati Five-Way Chili, 111–14

Fried Bologna Chili, 144–45

Homage to Hershey Chocolate Chili, 120–21

Serious Capitol Punishment Chili, 40–41

Church Supper Chili Mac and Cheese, 89–92

Cilantro

Mesilla Valley Bowl of Green, 100–3

Cincinnati Five-Way Chili, 111–14

Cocoa. *See* Chocolate/Cocoa

Code 10 Chili, 150–51

Coffee Chili, Seattle, 142–43

Coleslaw, 158

Cook-offs, 14–15

Cookware, 7

Corn

Bluegrass Burgoo Chili, 62–64

Blue Hen Succotash Chili, 38–39

Chili of the Garden State, 98–99

Corn Pudding, 156
Highway 61 Chili, 82–83
Jalapeño Corn Bread, 157
Navaho Lamb and Golden Hominy
    Chili, 134–35
Tall Corn Pork Chili, 56–57
Cornish Miner Chili Pasties, 75–77
Cornmeal
    Chicken, Chili and Cornmeal Parsley
        Dumplings, 122–24
    Hot Springs Chili-Tamale Spread,
        26–29
    Jalapeño Corn Bread, 157
Cowboy Poetry Chili, 93–94
Crabmeat
    Chesapeake Bay Chili, 71–72
Cranberry beans
    Maple-Spiked Chili with Cheddar
        Stars, 136–38
Cream Cheese Chili, Sonoran Pork,
    Poblano, and, 24–25
Creamy Grits, 126

D

Dumplings, Cornmeal Parsley, Chicken
    Chili and, 122–24

E

Eggplant
    Mardi Gras Vegetable Chili, 65–67

F

Forty Below Meat Loaf and Mashed
    Potatoes Chili, 108–10
Fried Bologna Chili, 144–45

Garlic Chili, Gilroy Super, 30–32
Georgia Pork and Peanut Chili, 44–45
Gilroy Super Garlic Chili, 30–32
Green Bay Chili, 146–49
Green beans
    Three-Bean Salad, 155
Green chiles. *See also* Chiles; *specific kinds*
    Code 10 Chili, 150–51
    Cornish Miner Chili Pasties, 75–77
    Herb Garden Springtime Chili,
        36–37
    Tall Corn Pork Chili, 56–57
Grits
    Low-Country Chicken Chili,
        125–27
Guacamole, Perfect Simple, 154

H

Habanero chiles, 12. *See also* Chiles
    Code 10 Chili, 150–51
    Navaho Lamb and Golden Hominy
        Chili, 134–35
Havana Moon Chili, 42–43
Herb Garden Springtime Chili, 36–37
Highway 61 Chili, 82–83
Homage to Hershey Chocolate Chili,
    120–21
Hominy
    Mardi Gras Vegetable Chili, 65–67
    Navaho Lamb and Golden Hominy
        Chili, 134–35
Horseradish
    Horseradish Pickles, 60–61
    Let 'er Buck Red Beef Chili, 118–19
Hot Springs Chili-Tamale Spread,
    26–29

I

International Chili Society, 14–15

J

Jalapeño peppers, 12
    Café Brenda Black Bean Vegetable
        Chili, 78–81
    Chili of the Garden State, 98–99
    Code 10 Chili, 150–51
    Jalapeño Corn Bread, 157

K

Kidney beans
    Chicagoland Chili Mac, 51–52
    Chili of the Garden State, 98–99
    Cincinnati Five-Way Chili, 111–14
    Fried Bologna Chili, 144–45
    Green Bay Chili, 146–49
    Homage to Hershey Chocolate Chili,
        120–21
    Low-Country Chicken Chili, 125–27
    Mardi Gras Vegetable Chili, 65–67
    Porubsky's Grocery Store Chili,
        58–61
    Three-Bean Salad, 155

L

Lamb
    Bluegrass Burgoo Chili, 62–64
    Cowboy Poetry Chili, 93–94
    Navajo Lamb and Golden Hominy
        Chili, 134–35
Let 'er Buck Red Beef Chili, 118–19
Lima beans
    Bluegrass Burgoo Chili, 62–64
    Blue Hen Succotash Chili, 38–39
Line Camp Chili and Biscuits, 21–23
Low-Country Chicken Chili, 125–27

M

Macadamia Nut and Chipotle Chili,
    Paniolo, 46–47
Macaroni
    American Chop Suey Chili, 68–70
    Chicagoland Chili Mac, 51–52
    Church Supper Chili Mac and Cheese,
        89–92
Mail-order sources, 8–10
Maple-Spiked Chili with Cheddar Stars,
    136–38
Mardi Gras Vegetable Chili, 65–67
Masa harina as thickener, 6
Mashed Potatoes, 109–10
Memphis Barbecue Shrimp Chili, 130–31
Mesilla Valley Bowl of Green, 100–3
Mule-Kicking Hot Chili, 84–85

N

Navaho Lamb and Golden Hominy Chili,
    134–35
New Mexico chiles, 13. *See also* Chiles
    Mesilla Valley Bowl of Green, 100–3
    Working Person's Green Chili Bowl,
        86–88
Nuts
    Georgia Pork and Peanut Chili, 44–45
    Havana Moon Chili, 42–43
    Paniolo Macadamia Nut and Chipotle
        Chili, 46–47
    Shenandoah Valley Apple-Nut Chili,
        139–41
    Oil, Spicy, 148–49

O

Okra
    Bluegrass Burgoo Chili, 62–64
Olives
    Havana Moon Chili, 42–43
    Oregano, about, 6

P

Paniolo Macadamia Nut and Chipotle Chili,
46–47
Parsley
Chicken Chili and Cornmeal Parsley
Dumplings, 122–24
Herb Garden Springtime Chili, 36–37
Mardi Gras Vegetable Chili, 65–67
Mesilla Valley Bowl of Green, 100–3
Paniolo Macadamia Nut and Chipotle
Chili, 46–47
Parsnips
Line Camp Chili and Biscuits, 21–23
Pasilla chiles, 13
Mule-Kicking Hot Chili, 84–85
Navaho Lamb and Golden Hominy
Chili, 134–35
Seattle Coffee Chili, 142–43
Shenandoah Valley Apple-Nut Chili,
139–41
Pasta
American Chop Suey Chili, 68–70
Chicagoland Chili Mac, 51–52
Church Supper Chili Mac and Cheese,
89–92
Cincinnati Five-Way Chili, 111–14
Green Bay Chili, 146–49
Pasties, Cornish Miner Chili, 75–77
Peanuts/Peanut butter
Georgia Pork and Peanut Chili,
44–45
Shenandoah Valley Apple-Nut Chili,
139–41
Peeling tomatoes, 7
Peppers. See Bell peppers; Chiles; specific
kinds
Perfect Simple Guacamole, 154
Pickles, Horseradish, 60–61
Pig Chili, 106–7
Pink beans. *See also* Beans, canned or dried
Cowboy Poetry Chili, 93–94

Pinto beans. *See also* Beans, canned or dried
Chili à la Whistle Stop, 18–20
Hot Springs Chili-Tamale Spread,
26–29
Low-Country Chicken Chili, 125–27
Roughneck Boilermaker Chili,
128–29
Poblano chiles, 13. *See also* Chiles
Sonoran Pork, Poblano, and Cream
Cheese Chili, 24–25
Pork. *See also* Salt pork
Georgia Pork and Peanut Chili, 44–45
ground
Forty Below Meat Loaf and
Mashed Potatoes Chili, 108–10
Havana Moon Chili, 42–43
Highway 61 Chili, 82–83
Serious Capitol Punishment
Chili, 40–41
Paniolo Macadamia Nut and Chipotle
Chili, 46–47
Pig Chili, 106–7
sausage
Bluegrass Burgoo Chili, 62–64
Code 10 Chili, 150–51
Venison Chili with Snowcap
Beans, 33–35
Shenandoah Valley Apple-Nut Chili,
139–41
Sonoran Pork, Poblano, and Cream
Cheese Chili, 24–25
Tall Corn Pork Chili, 56–57
Working Person's Green Chili Bowl,
86–88
Porubsky's Grocery Store Chili, 58–61
Potatoes
Chili Coeur d'Alene, 48–50
Code 10 Chili, 150–51
Cornish Miner Chili Pasties, 75–77
Forty Below Meat Loaf and Mashed
Potatoes Chili, 108–10
Sunday Supper Chicken Chili, 53–55

Pudding, Corn, 156
Pumpkin seeds
    Café Brenda Black Bean Vegetable
        Chili, 78–81

Q

Quick-soak method for beans, 5

R

Raisins
    Havana Moon Chili, 42–43
Rehydrating dried peppers, 4–5
Roadhouse Barbecue Sauce, 6–7
Roasting peppers, 5–6
Rock-Ribbed Bean-and-Beef Chili, 73–74
Roughneck Boilermaker Chili, 128–29

S

Salads
    Coleslaw, 158
    Three-Bean, 155
Salt pork
    Yankee Bean Pot Chili, 95–97
Sandwiches
    Buffalo Beef and Weck Chili, 104–5
Sausage
    Bluegrass Burgoo Chili, 62–64
    Code 10 Chili, 150–51
    Mule-Kicking Hot Chili, 84–85
    Venison Chili with Snowcap Beans,
        33–35
Scallions
    Chicken Chili and Cornmeal Parsley
        Dumplings, 122–24
    Hot Springs Chili-Tamale Spread,
        26–29
    Shenandoah Apple-Nut Chili, 139–41

Seattle Coffee Chili, 142–43
Serious Capitol Punishment Chili, 40–41
Shenandoah Valley Apple-Nut Chili,
    139–41
Shrimp
    Chesapeake Bay Chili, 71–72
    Memphis Barbecue Shrimp Chili,
        130–31
    Side dishes
    Coleslaw, 158
    Corn Pudding, 156
    Jalapeño Corn Bread, 157
    Perfect Simple Guacamole, 154
    Three–Bean Salad, 155
16-Times World Champion Sirloin Chili,
    115–17
Snowcap Beans, Venison Chili with, 33–35
Soaking beans, 5
Sonoran Pork, Poblano, and Cream Cheese
    Chili, 24–25
Spaghetti
    Cincinnati Five-Way Chili-, 111–14
    Green Bay Chili, 146–49
Spicy Oil, 148–49
Sunday Supper Chicken Chili, 53–55

T

Tall Corn Pork Chili, 56–57
Tamale Spread, Hot Springs Chili-, 26–29
Three-Bean Salad, 155
Tigua Indian Definitive Bowl of Red,
    132–33
Tomatillos
    about, 7
    Cowboy Poetry Chili, 93–94
    Gilroy Super Garlic Chili, 30–32
    Herb Garden Springtime Chili, 36–37
    Mesilla Valley Bowl of Green, 100–3
Tomatoes. *See also* Tomato Sauce
    American Chop Suey Chili, 68–70

Bluegrass Burgoo Chili, 62–64
Blue Hen Succotash Chili, 38–39
Chicagoland Chili Mac, 51–52
Chili Coeur d'Alene, 48–50
Chili of the Garden State, 98–99
Chili à la Whistle Stop, 18–20
Church Supper Chili Mac and Cheese,
　89–92
Fried Bologna Chili, 144–45
Havana Moon Chili, 42–43
Highway 61 Chili, 82–83
Low-Country Chicken Chili, 125–27
Maple-Spiked Chili with Cheddar
　Stars, 136–38
Mardi Gras Vegetable Chili, 65–67
Navaho Lamb and Golden Hominy
　Chili, 134–35
peeling, 7
Pig Chili, 106–7
Rock-Ribbed Bean-and-Beef Chili,
　73–74
Roughneck Boilermaker Chili,
　128–29
Serious Capitol Punishment Chili,
　40–41
Sunday Supper Chicken Chili, 53–55
Venison Chili with Snowcap Beans,
　33–35
Tomato sauce
　Bluegrass Burgoo Chili, 62–64
　Chicagoland Chili Mac, 51–52
　Chili à Whistle Stop, 18–20
　Cornish Miner Chili Pasties, 75–77
　Forty Below Meat Loaf and Mashed
　　Potatoes Chili, 108–10

Georgia Pork and Peanut Chili, 44–45
Highway 61 Chili, 82–83
Let 'er Buck Red Beef Chili, 118–19
Line Camp Chili and Biscuits, 21–23
Porubsky's Grocery Store Chili,
　58–61
16-Times World Champion Sirloin
　Chili, 115–17
Tall Corn Pork Chili, 56–57
Tigua Indian Definitive Bowl of Red,
　132–33
Turnips
　Cornish Miner Chili Pasties, 75–77

V

Veal, ground
　Forty Below Meat Loaf and Mashed
　　Potatoes Chili, 108–10
Venison Chili with Snowcap Beans, 33–35

W

Whiskey
　Roughneck Boilermaker Chili,
　　128–29
Working Person's Green Chili Bowl, 86–88

Y

Yankee Bean Pot Chili, 95–97
Yellow-eyed beans. See also Beans, canned
　or dried
　　Yankee Bean Pot Chili, 95–97